Winning Without a
CHAMPIONSHIP

LESSONS LEARNED FROM
A NON-CHAMPIONSHIP COACH

JASON BORNN

KP PUBLISHING COMPANY

Copyright 2023 by Jason Bornn

Winning Without A Championship: Lessons Learned from a Non-Championship Coach

All rights reserved. In accordance with the U.S. Copyright Act of 1976, the scanning, uploading, and electronic sharing of any part of this book without the permission of the publisher is unlawful piracy and theft of the author's intellectual property. If you would like to use material from this book (other than for review purposes), prior written permission must be obtained by contacting the publisher at info@kp-pub.com

Thank you for your support of the author's rights.

ISBN: 978-1-960001-43-6 (Paperback)
ISBN: 978-1-960001-44-3 (Ebook)

Library of Congress Control Number: Pending

Editor: Frank D. Williams
Cover Design: Juan Roberts, Creative Lunacy
Literary Director: Sandra Slayton James

All Bible scriptures are from the King James Version.

Published by:

KP Publishing Company
Publisher of Fiction, Nonfiction & Children's Books
Valencia, CA 91355
www.kp-pub.com

Printed in the United States of America

CONTENTS

Dedication		*vii*
Introduction		*ix*
Chapter 1	Mentors: People Who Shaped My Ideas	1
Chapter 2	13-Year Assistant Coach: Lessons Learned from the Trenches	25
Chapter 3	1st Year as a Head Coach: What Worked, What Didn't	53
Chapter 4	Building a Culture: Vision, Mission, Core Beliefs	75
Chapter 5	Pyramid of Success: Offense and Defense	97
Chapter 6	Assistant Coaches: Only the Few	117
Chapter 7	Working With Parents: It Takes a Village	135
Chapter 8	Leadership Principles: What It Takes to Lead as a Coach and Player	151
Chapter 9	Winning the Wrong Way: What's Really Important in Coaching	165
Chapter 10	Keeping a Balance: Faith, Family, Football	177
Chapter 11	Coaching Your Own Children: Nothing Better, Nothing More Challenging	187

Chapter 12	Dealing with 21st Century Culture: Issues of Today	199
Chapter 13	Tragedy and Triumph: School Shooting, COVID-19, and League Champs	209
Chapter 14	Where Do We Go from Here: Moving Forward?	223
Chapter 15	Epilogue	227

Acknowledgment	*233*
About the Author	*237*
Appendix	*239*

DEDICATION

This work is dedicated to my bride, Veronica, whose continuous love, support, and encouragement made this book possible. I would also like to recognize my three children, Angelo, Julian, and Paloma, for blessing me with the opportunity to be their dad.

INTRODUCTION

Winning Without A Championship Lessons learned from a non-championship coach

The vast majority of coaches across all sports do not win championships. However, our culture gravitates towards teams that do, often disregarding the lessons learned by those who have not. This book shares lessons, ideas, and concepts I have learned through coaching football over the course of my career, with very few championships.

My experience has given me ways to affect young lives beyond winning a championship. Some of the content in this book may seem like common sense to the general reader. However, my experience has shown me that what may seem like common sense is often overlooked or simply ignored. My goal is to compile a no-frills, easy-to-understand method for succeeding and winning. The key was to avoid typical championship pursuits. Winning several championships isn't always workable, so we must pursue success through other means. This work strives to do that.

Let me clarify: this isn't a book on football. Yes, the lessons I have learned are based on my own experiences as a high school football coach. However, I feel they apply to anyone who wants to be successful in whatever avenue of life they pursue. My intention is for each chapter to be a stand-alone talking point, covering what worked and what didn't. These lessons apply to any profession. This work provides an alternative outlook on winning without a championship.

In Chapter 1, I will recount all the mentors who have and continue to shape my thought process in guiding our program over the course of my career. This list is not absolute and is ongoing. I believe it lays the groundwork for much of what I have learned and continue to develop. In Chapters 2 and 3, I go over the lessons learned as an assistant football coach and a first-year head coach. These experiences have allowed me to develop and grow as a professional and on a personal level. Chapters 4 and 5 focus on specific ways and ideas on how to create a culture that works for you in whatever area of your life you choose. While it may appear to be football-centric, the blueprint allows anyone to tailor it to their needs. Chapters 6 and 7 focus on working with others, be it coworkers, subordinates, or others who are vital to your area of life. Chapters 8 and 9 center on leadership, both the right and wrong ways to lead. In Chapter 10, I delve into the concept of having a balance in your life, which, if not maintained, will make everything you do come apart. Chapter 11 focuses on the idea of parenting your own children while they are engaged in sports. This chapter provides guidance on coaching children in sports. Chapter 12 delves into 21st-century issues I feel are paramount for us to acknowledge and address with our young people. Finally, Chapters 13 and 14 recount many of the lessons learned and described in the previous chapters.

My goal is for you to walk away from this book with one thing that you can apply to your own life. Be it with your profession, community, family, or any other area of your life, makes no difference to me. While I intended to provide lessons learned from my experiences that may help you, it is critical to point out that I am still a work in progress and not complete. This work was as much of a learning experience for me writing it as I hope it will be for you reading it.

Finally, thank you for taking the time to pick this up and read it. I hope you have as much fun reading this book as I did writing this, but more than anything else, I hope you walk away with ideas on how to be a winner without winning a championship!

1

MENTORS: PEOPLE WHO SHAPED MY IDEAS

"You only get out of it what you put into it."

—Drill Instructor Sergeant Z, USMC

Mentors. When I hear that word, I think of people who help others grow. It's a word that has always been interesting to me. It meant that someone else was investing their time, energy, and passion into you, if for no other reason just out of the goodness of their heart. This concept was one I had a hard time grasping growing up simply because I had very few mentors. Sure, I had friends, both young and old, who served as influences in my life, but as far as adults, who invested energy into me for growth, not so much. As I got older, I understood the purpose, intent, and value of mentors. The point I truly embraced was growth from those whose sole purpose was to increase knowledge, wisdom, and improvement for others. It was with this understanding that I reflected on my life and truly saw all the mentors I have had and how each of them contributed to the person I am today. It is why I am starting this book off with this topic: I recognize how invaluable mentors are to personal growth.

While this is not a memoir, I think it is important to give a little background on myself to ensure that the reader has a basic understanding of where I am coming from. I was born in Queens, NY, where I lived with my mother for about a year until she moved us to California. My dad, whom my mom was not married to, came out to California with her, but they did not stay together long (I have never met my dad to date). Shortly after, my mom married my stepdad, who had a daughter from a previous marriage. Together, they had my younger sister, and we were a family until I was the age of 11, at which time they divorced. My older stepsister had long moved out while my mom, younger sister, and I moved to a townhome. Once there, I began attending Village Christian Schools, a small private school in the San Fernando Valley, just north of Los Angeles. It was here that I began playing youth football, which transitioned into playing at the high school. I loved everything about the sport. The physicality of it, the long steamy practices, the passing league tournaments, and ultimately, Friday night football. By my senior year (1989), I recognized that, like so many other high school athletes, playing football in college was probably not going to happen. I then enlisted in the Marine Corps, where I served for six years as a reservist with the 3rd ANGLICO in Long Beach, California. My goal after boot camp and military occupation specialty training was to go to college, earn my degree, and apply to law enforcement agencies. The goal was to have a long career as a police officer.

Following my military training, I would return to my high school to visit my former football coach. While visiting with Coach Plaisance, he offered me an opportunity to coach that season at my alma mater. I never thought of coaching, but with my playing days done, I saw it as a great way to stay involved with the game while studying and working towards becoming a police officer. Never in a million years could I have imagined that 31 years later, I would still be a high school football coach.

After that first season, I was hooked. It was then that I pursued a degree in history so that I could be a teacher, which would allow me the opportunity to coach full-time. I had no intention of getting into education, let alone being a high school history teacher.

Upon graduation from California State University Northridge in 1995, I got my degree in history and completed my teaching credential. After serving six years as the defensive coordinator at Village (1990-1995), I would move on to John Muir High School in Pasadena. The legendary Jackie Robinson attended here. I worked at Muir as an assistant coach for five seasons (1996-2000). Following that, I served one year at Canyon High School in Canyon Country, California (2001), followed by a year working at Occidental College (2002). I would then work for a short off-season at Notre Dame High School of Sherman Oaks, California, in the spring of 2003. After this, they gave me the opportunity to be the head coach at my current school, Saugus High School, in 2003.

Along this journey, there have been plenty of mentors who helped shape me into the coach I am today. I am sure there are many more, but the following people are the ones who left the most lasting impact and have given me knowledge that I feel is important.

MY MOM

I can't begin this discussion without starting with my mom. She is hands down the smartest, toughest, and most honest person I know. As a single mom, from the time I was 11, she worked hard to provide for me and my younger sister. She worked in the aerospace industry, making enough money to not only provide a roof over our heads but to send us both to a private school. What I learned from watching my mom was to not dwell on the challenges, setbacks, and tragedies of life. She had a tough upbringing, but you would never know it because she never really talked about it. She got up each day, got ready for work, and did what she needed to do. This instilled in me a sense of moving on and getting things done, regardless of what life throws at you. She never whined, complained, or wallowed in her past, nor did she get sidetracked by whatever challenges hit her at the moment. She just kept going, period. Some may say that this quality of not discussing or talking about life's challenges is unhealthy. Maybe for some, it is, but for her, what I saw was a sign of strength and determination in the face of adversity. This would be very impactful to me as I faced various challenges in my life.

Another lesson I learned from my mom was the idea of responsibility and ownership. One year, while a freshman in high school, I got a D on my report card. I remember thinking at the time that she would be mad and ground me over it. But her response was one I was not expecting. After looking at the report card, she simply said that the grade I got was my grade, not hers. She said that she had already graduated from high school and college and that the only person being hurt by me not getting good grades was me. She then said that no matter what grades I got or what I did beyond high school, she would love me unconditionally. But she stressed that the grades I got and the choices I made were exactly that—mine. This lesson really stuck with me. It showed me that the decisions and choices I make are 100% on me. It really drove the point home that anything I do in life is on me.

The last lesson I credit my mom with is the idea of following your passions, regardless of money. When deciding to pursue a career in teaching, I had serious reservations about it because of the low pay teachers make. Not that I was concerned about making a ton of money, but I wanted to make enough money to have nice things and be able to support myself and a future family. I had always heard that teaching was a profession you don't get into to make money but to make a difference in young people's lives.

While that alone was worth it, as a nineteen-year-old about to embark on his life's profession, my maturity level was such that money was an important factor. I went to my mom with my concerns, and she simply said, "Don't worry about the money. Follow your passions, and the money will take care of itself." That simple piece of advice made all the difference. She stressed there are a lot of people who make a lot of money but are miserable going to a job they hate. To me, that made no sense since you spend the bulk of your day at work. Sure, you could have a nice car, home, all kinds of toys, vacations, etc., etc., but who cares if you have all those things if you dread going to work? I took her advice and went into teaching/coaching, and it's made all the difference.

COACH MIKE PLAISANCE, HEAD COACH, VILLAGE CHRISTIAN HIGH SCHOOL, SUN VALLEY, CALIFORNIA, PART 1

Once in high school, I began playing football, making the JV team in both my freshman and sophomore years. Each of those first two seasons, I sustained injuries (a torn ACL my first, a broken back my second) that kept me off the field for the entire season. By my junior year, I was chomping at the bit to play and prove that I was not injury-prone. It was that year I began playing for Coach Plaisance, our varsity head football coach.

Coach Plaisance was a former star quarterback who was the 1965 Louisiana State Player of the Year out of St. Augustine High School in New Orleans. His life dream was to play college football for LSU. However, being a black athlete in the South during the 1960s, he could not attend the storied institution because school integration had not happened. It was at this point in his life that he realized his race had restricted his opportunities. He made the choice to pursue his life's dream of playing college football somewhere else. Coach Plaisance attended the Historically Black College and University (HBCU) of Grambling State University. The institution was a football powerhouse. While not his first choice, he would play for the legendary Eddie Robinson, who at the time had the most wins in college football history. After some success in the early years of college, someone injured him his senior year, which ended his career and ability to play professionally. It was at this point that he went into education and ended up in California as a teacher and coach.

Once I began playing for him, I quickly realized that he was much more than just my coach. He became a father figure to me. He coached all of us, but I felt like we had a special relationship (my senior year, I even had his last name on the back of my jersey instead of my own). His passion for the game was clear in his preparation for our opponents, but he always took the time to talk to us on a much deeper level about life. His stories of growing up in the Deep South gave us a better understanding of race relations and an appreciation of how truly blessed we were. I would seek his advice about various things going on in my life, and he was always available to talk to me. His perspective was different and real. He would not sugarcoat things and was always honest. I learned from him that a coach could and should be more than just a coach. He laid the framework I would use throughout my coaching career to make deeper connections with the players. Sure, a line needed to be established so that you could get the players to do things that needed to be done, but it balanced this with being a mentor.

Another thing I learned from playing under Coach Plaisance was how to create a team of guys who were extremely close on and off the field. He would ensure that we were a team that loved each other and would do whatever it took to help each other out. He created this environment. We took part in activities we would do as a team, such as social gatherings outside of practice, team meals, and non-football-related events. To this day, many of the guys that I played high school football with are close friends of mine today. Sure, we have all gotten older and moved to different parts of California and other states, but we stay connected. I credit this to the atmosphere that Coach Plaisance created for us. We have used this concept with every team I have coached since. We have made it a priority to make our teams close by doing team bonding activities and promoting the idea of brotherhood that will last a lifetime.

USMC DRILL INSTRUCTOR SERGEANT Z, MCRD, SAN DIEGO, CALIFORNIA.

Upon graduation from high school, I entered the United States Marine Corps. I would leave for boot camp at MCRD (Marine Corps Recruit Depot) in San Diego, California, in the fall of 1989. Upon arrival, I immediately questioned the decision I had made to join the Corps. Yelling and screaming were constant. The relentless pace of training was never-ending. With the constant fear of doing things wrong, I was completely overwhelmed by the Marine Corps training. But with each passing day, I adjusted to the routine of becoming a Marine. One reason was because of our drill instructors, one in particular.

When a person joins the Marines, they place you in a platoon for training, with anywhere from 80 to 120 other recruits, under a cadre of drill instructors known as DIs, who lead training. Each platoon has a Senior DI who serves as the leader of the other DIs and acts almost like a father figure. Next in charge is called a lead instructor DI, then a heavy DI, and usually one or two more DIs who are in training. The heavy DI's sole mission is to cause fear and trepidation among the recruits. They usually make yelling and screaming an art form. The lead instructor, while still scary, serves as the leader of instruction on everything that is a Marine. Our lead instructor was Sergeant Z.

Sergeant Z was what we call a very squared-away Marine. Not that the other DIs weren't, but Sergeant Z's uniform always seemed to be crisper and cleaner looking than the others. While his demeanor was ramrod straight and stern, he was a teacher. He took the time to explain what needed to be done, from how to shine our boots to cleaning our weapons. While this was invaluable to us young recruits, it was his bedtime talks that stood out to me more than anything else.

At night, Sergeant Z would patrol the squad bay, giving inspiring speeches. He would say things that seemed to lift our spirits after a hard day of training. He would remind us that no matter how much we messed up during the day, we were on track to becoming Marines if we didn't quit and learned from our mistakes. For me, his words were always a welcome reprieve from the yelling and screaming that we all endured throughout the day. I found this very useful in the years to come as a coach. No matter how hard practice was or how much you yelled at them, you must bring them together at the end and give them something positive to walk away with.

Finally, one statement that Sergeant Z said one night while walking the squad bay has stuck with me all these years later. He said, "No one forced you to sign a contract to become a Marine. This was your choice. You might as well give everything you got to this training. You only get out of it what you put into it." It was this last statement that resonated with me. I have tried to be "all in" in everything I do. When you break it down, nothing could be truer. Whatever you decide to do, you must make the choice to give it your all so that you can get all that comes with being 100% committed. You can't expect to have greatness if you're not willing to do all you can to give it your best.

COACH MIKE PLAISANCE, HEAD COACH, VILLAGE CHRISTIAN HIGH SCHOOL, SUN VALLEY, CALIFORNIA, PART 2

Once I began coaching for Coach Plaisance, our dynamic only continued to grow, but this time as an assistant. He brought me on as the defensive coordinator, which, as a 19-year-old, was a lot of responsibility. I had assistant coaches working with me on the defensive staff. Some of them were several years older than me, but the final decisions regarding defense fell on me. While working with him for six seasons, I learned the value of practice organization and pride and ownership in your work.

I remember how organized our practices were by the plan he would create for us each day of practice. This was before the time of computers, so each plan was handwritten. I adhered to the plan without exception. It thoroughly explained each part of the practice. Stretching to conditioning, from individual periods to offense, defense, and special teams. This taught me that time was valuable. You had to ensure that you stuck to the plan so that the things we needed to work on got done while making sure we weren't there for four hours. It didn't matter if I had finished going over what I needed during my time. If it was time to move on, we moved on. This forced me to make sure that I was very detail-oriented and used my time wisely. This was an invaluable lesson that I took with me wherever I coached.

As the defensive coordinator, I was in charge of everything related to defense. This meant I had scouted the opponent, creating a plan to stop the opposing team's offense, and implemented the plan for practice. This required a lot of time and effort. It also meant that everything regarding stopping the other team's offense fell on me. This was a lot to take on, especially those first couple of years. While I loved the game, I was still very young and had a lot to learn. I read a lot of books, spoke to a lot of coaches, and attended as many clinics as I could to learn everything possible about defense. This created a tremendous amount of pride and ownership in my work. I broke down our opponents and did the best I could to create a game plan. The goal was to take away what they did best on offense. We wanted to get our players who played on the defense to take a lot of pride in their work and prepare for the opponent's offense. This was our means of executing a game plan on game day. It required that our players understood what to do on each call and that we all understood what the offense was trying to do. Taking pride and ownership in one's work is invaluable. When you know that it ultimately all falls on you, there is a whole new level of preparation that is required, and I relished in it.

Finally, I learned how to run a program with class. Coach Plaisance was always nice to the officials before the game, chatting it up with them and treating them with respect. It went a long way during a game, especially when calls did not go our way. With the support of people in the program, he always acknowledged them and said thank you for helping. This included the chain gang working our sideline, teachers on campus working with the students, or custodians and office managers. Coach was always thanking them and treating them as if they were part of the program. From game day programs, press guides, and putting on end-of-the-season banquets, he always did things with class. For a small school, we always had nice things and showed a genuine sense of community and family with anyone involved in the program. These were lessons I took with me wherever I coached.

COACH BILL WILLIAMS, FCPGA, POWAY, CALIFORNIA

When I started coaching with Coach Plaiance, I realized I had a lot to learn in terms of the fundamentals and techniques of coaching football. I began attending coaching clinics, which introduced me to a whole new world of the game. These clinics covered various topics, from schemes on offense, defense, and special teams to the smallest details of how to coach specific positions and run a successful program. No other person has had more influence on me to coach the specific fundamentals of all positions than Coach Williams.

Coach Williams was a former coach at both the high school and collegiate level who got into the business of coaching coaches. Based out of Poway, California, Coach Williams put on clinics like some of the other companies that were doing the same thing. He covered a variety of topics, but it was his smaller, specialized clinics that attracted me the most. I attended several of them through his company, the Football Coaches Professional Growth Association. He presented topics on blocking and tackling. Inside linebacker fundamentals was another one. He did several on special teams. When one attended these smaller clinics, attendance spots were limited. We would travel to a hotel in Poway and completely immerse ourselves in the topic covered. It literally started Friday evening, rolled into all day on Saturday until late at night, and finished mid-Sunday afternoon. By the time you left, you were both mentally and physically exhausted, but you had learned more than you could imagine.

What separated his clinics from others was that we were required to do the drills, "chalk talk" it out on dry-erase boards, and watch hours of film on whatever the topic was.

What I learned from Coach Williams was how to take a fundamental technique and completely deconstruct it into the smallest, simplest parts. Using the term "bird dog," we would literally take one step at a time in learning and teaching techniques. He would often teach in reverse, meaning we would start with the end in mind and work backward to the beginning. It was an incredibly effective way to teach. We would finish the technique by doing what he referred to as the "whole enchilada," putting all the steps together. Again, this was a completely new way to teach the game that someone had never exposed me to, but it made me a much better teacher of the game. I will always have a special place in my heart for Coach Williams and what he taught me.

COACH TOM OSBORNE, HEAD COACH, UNIVERSITY OF NEBRASKA

As a young coach, I began studying successful football coaches from all levels. I wanted to get as much information as possible regarding what it took to be successful on and off the field. One coach that I studied in the 1990s was Coach Osborne, the head football coach at the University of Nebraska.

Nebraska football was one of the dominant sports teams of any level during the 1990s. They had won a ton of games and seemed to reload year after year. What intrigued me the most about the program was their coach, Coach Osborne. I began reading as many books as possible on Coach Osborne as I could find. As I devoured these books, what became abundantly clear to me was his program encompassed character development. He spent as much time on developing the character of his players as he did on the X's and O's of the game. A major part of his character development was based on his Christian faith. He invested heavily in his players' personal lives. He handled any challenges they may have been having with compassion and understanding. Part of this process involved the creation of a unity council. This allowed him to have a better understanding of what the players were dealing with, as well as addressing any team-related issues. This unity council comprised players from different grade levels, backgrounds, positions, and personalities. By having a variety of players take part, he could have a pretty good understanding and feel for the pulse of the team. He would use this unity council to drive home his character education and indoctrination. I found this fascinating because not only was he staying abreast of the current climate of his team, but he was also developing team leadership skills as well. I knew that if I was ever a head coach, I would do something similar.

COACH JIM BROWNFIELD, HEAD COACH, JOHN MUIR HIGH SCHOOL, PASADENA, CALIFORNIA

I had been coaching at my alma mater for six seasons when I finished my bachelor's degree in history and teaching credential. Unfortunately, they did not have a teaching job for me, so I began looking at other local high schools for employment. It introduced me to Coach Brownfield, the former head coach at John Muir in Pasadena. I had played with his one nephew in high school and coached the other while at Village. He was a legend in the football community, having led Muir to two CIF championships in the mid-'80s. When I met him, I could not believe how much energy he had for someone who had retired from both teaching and coaching. He was extremely active in the football community, especially with the National Football Foundation and College Hall of Fame. From day one, he put me to work in the foundation, performing a variety of tasks. What I learned from Coach Brownfield was attention to detail about all aspects of running a program. He had put together a manual of all the things needed to run not only a team but also a complete program. He had things in his manual that never even crossed my mind. Organizational structure was his strength, and he made sure that everything on campus connected to the program. From the band to ASB, to school administration, to feeder programs, he built his program so that everyone was a part of it. It overwhelmed my mind with the amount of work he put into running the program. There were things he did I would never have thought about doing. It would serve me well in the years to come.

Another thing that Coach Brownfield did was introduce me to John Wooden's Pyramid of Success. I was not much of a basketball fan, so this was the first time I had ever heard about Coach Wooden and UCLA basketball. He sat down with me and went over every aspect of the Pyramid. It showed me that to be successful, every detail needs to be implemented and explained to not only the players but anyone associated with the program. I found it very enlightening and educational and would use it to structure several areas of my future programs.

Finally, Coach Brownfield introduced me to the then-current head coaches at Muir, Tony Crutchfield and Erik Johnson, who were serving as co-head coaches of the school. Once I met them, they hired me to coach on their staff. Once school started, I was hired as a social studies teacher in the fall of 1996.

Mentors: People Who Shaped My Ideas

COACH ERIK JOHNSON, HEAD COACH, JOHN MUIR HIGH SCHOOL, PASADENA, CALIFORNIA

That first season at Muir was a culture shock. I came from a small private Christian school whose student body was predominantly white. Muir, a much larger public school, had a student population that was Hispanic and Black. It was exciting to work with players who were being nationally recruited. As the only coach on campus (both Coach Crutchfield and Coach Johnson were walk-ons), I was the one who met with college coaches seeking information about our players. It was a very exciting time. After two seasons, Coach Crutchfield moved on, and Coach Johnson became the sole head coach in 1998. Coach Johnson came to me and said that he wanted me to run the defense but had one stipulation: it had to be a 3-4 defense. When I ran the defense at Village, we ran a 44 defense (aka, 4-2-5 in today's parlance), and Coach Crutchfield ran a similar defense my first two seasons at Muir. It forced me to learn all I could about the system.

Coach Johnson was obsessed with knowing why you do what you do. He wanted me to have all the answers for everything related to the defense. If I didn't know the answer, he made me seek people out who did. I read books, reached out to coaches, and attended clinics, all in a quest to become competent in coordinating this new defense.

We learned a completely new system and thrived in the constant dialog the two of us had in ensuring that we knew all the strengths and weaknesses of the defense. I learned to tear it down, attack it, and find solutions to fix it when things went wrong (i.e., when and what adjustments to make). Coach Johnson was a master at asking questions that really forced me to know why I was doing what I was doing. It made me do my homework to ensure that I knew my stuff. I will long remember those discussions we had, figuring out all the finer points of the defense. The lesson I took from Coach Johnson was to really break things down and know the why behind it, but probably the most important lesson was how to fix it when things went south.

Finally, I learned the idea of having players take multiple reps in practice. Nothing drove him crazier than having one player doing a drill while others stood around and watched or waited their turn. Time was always an issue, and he wanted to ensure that we maximized it as much as possible. He was adamant about having drills done in mass so that each player could get as many reps as doing the task (s) asked of them. The idea was a great one in that it ensured players were constantly in motion and getting to work. I loved this concept and carried it with me to each coaching stop I had along the way.

COACH BOB LADOUCEUR, HEAD COACH, DE LA SALLE HIGH SCHOOL, CONCORD, CALIFORNIA

While I was coaching at Muir, I continued to study successful coaches from all levels. One that really struck an interest in me was Coach Ladouceur, the head football coach at De La Salle High School in Concord, California. His program had an amazing win streak. Eventually, it would end at 151 games after losing to Bellevue High School in Washington in 2004. This garnered national attention, but it was the way their teams played that piqued my interest. I began reading every book and watching every documentary on them I could find, as well as recording their games on TV. I studied their precision and execution on offense, their stout play on defense, and their creativity on special teams. But a couple of things that really stuck out to me was the way he ran the program. He seemed to get his players to play on a completely different level. They not only executed their system like a machine, but they also played for the love of their teammates. In the books and documentaries

I found, I realized he did things to get his players to work harder than anyone they played, and their play showed that.

The other thing that stood out to me was their team meals, which were held each Thursday night before game day. It was at these team meals that players wrote out commitment cards that were then shared with other teammates. I loved the idea that players committed practice and game goals to each other and ensured that they held each other accountable for what they wrote and spoke. This idea seemed unique to me in that they were having the players take ownership of what they said they were going to do. It was something that I would use when I became a head coach.

Finally, I had the chance to meet Coach Ladouceur face-to-face in the early 2000s at a coaching clinic in Southern California. I had reached out to him ahead of time and asked if we could meet after his speaking session was done. My goal was to ask him questions about running a program, balancing home and work (which will be discussed in a later chapter), and finally, how to coach. One thing that he stressed was that you had to give your players constant feedback after each rep of a drill, group period, or team period. His idea was that players need that information after every rep so that they know exactly what to do to improve. His theory was that, as a coach, you should be mentally exhausted after practice because you were so focused on giving the players constant feedback. He gave me some other expert advice, but the thing I remember most was him saying, "You can win and do it the wrong way." That statement really stuck with me. To me, it meant that winning, while important, is not the end all be all. You can still have success, regardless of the scoreboard.

COACH HARRY WELCH, HEAD COACH, CANYON HIGH SCHOOL, CANYON COUNTRY, CALIFORNIA

In 2001, I joined the Canyon High School coaching staff of Coach Welch. It was Coach Welch's second tenure as head coach of the Cowboys. He had previously coached in the late 1970s through 1993, winning 3 CIF (California Interscholastic Federation) championships in a row (1983-85). At one point, his teams had a 46-game win streak. He had stepped down as head coach in the early 1990s and returned to the program's helm for the 2001 season.

I first learned of Coach Welch while still in high school. His teams were physical and disciplined. I saw a couple of their games later when I started coaching and walked away feeling the same way about their teams. Coach Brownfield from Muir often talked about "The King," as he often referred to him, and how much he admired Coach Welch and how he ran his program. So, when I could work on his staff, I jumped at the chance.

Once on his staff, we began preparation for the 2001 campaign with coaches' meetings in January 2001. From day one, he impressed me with his straightforward approach to coaching the game. He stressed that the blueprint for success was toughness, fundamentals, and strict adherence to the "Cowboy Way." The "Cowboy Way" was a simple set of standards by which everything was to be done. Whether in the weight room, doing sprints, or during practice, this standard was to be adhered to without exception. If Coach Welch said you were to start your sprint with your toe touching the line, that's precisely what everyone did. If even one player did not do this, we held everyone accountable, either doing some "reminding" (usually up-downs) or doing it repeatedly. We would do whatever the standard was until everyone got it right.

We began working with the players during our late winter/early spring PE period. It was the only way we could work with the football players doing football-specific training. We would never get to coaching actual football fundamentals. We would start with on-the-field practice from 2 to 3 pm each day and then hit the weight room from 3 to 5 pm. During the on-the-field portion, all we did was establish and reinforce the standard. It took place while stretching and sprinting until everyone did it right. If the players didn't do it right, we would start over. In those first few weeks, we did not do any actual football fundamentals because we would run out of time due to establishing and reinforcing the standards.

As a younger coach, I was eager to teach the fundamentals of the game as soon as possible. Coach Welch was adamant that we would only move on once we met the standard in the other areas. He insisted that this would translate later when we could coach the techniques needed for the players to play their respective positions. He was right. When we began coaching position-specific fundamentals, the players executed the fundamentals to precision. It was because we set the standard, and they followed it without question. This concept of setting the bar is challenging. As coaches, we often want to get to the sexy part of coaching (translation scheme) and forgo establishing standards for the team and each position. But when you develop the criteria first, your team and players will be much more prepared and will succeed at their positions when we demand this of them.

The other lesson I learned from Coach Welch was this: fundamentals and technique are far more critical than a scheme. When we began that season in 2001, we struggled to a 3-7 record. I remember thinking that the game had passed Coach Welch by and he was outdated. Not that what we were doing was bad, but it felt like perhaps our offense and defense were stuck in the 1980s. I sat down with Coach Welch at the end of the season to debrief with him about my observations over the season and a list of questions I wanted to ask. We never got past the first question (I don't even remember what it was). Coach was direct and honest with his answers toward me and continued to express other concepts that I needed to be more mature as a coach to understand and accept. I remember walking away from that meeting disappointed. There was no way the team would have any success if things continued being run the way they were. The schemes we were using needed to be updated and would never work. At this point, I decided to pursue other coaching opportunities. I moved on to coach DBs at Occidental College for the 2002 season. It wasn't too long after that when Coach Welch proved me wrong.

After I left Canyon, the team began an incredible run of winning. Each season, the program won more games. In 2005, they won the CIF Southern Section Championship. They then followed that up by winning their second CIF Championship in 2006. His team would go on to the first-ever CIF State Championship game, defeating Concord De La Salle High School in 2006. What amazed me the most was that Coach Welch's teams ran the same offense and defense as he did when I was on his staff. His devout attention to the intricacies of the fundamentals needed for each position to be successful was the key to success. This revealed that it's not the scheme that wins games but the strict adherence to each position's techniques and fundamentals that allows teams to succeed while on the field. Finally, Coach Welch further advanced this concept by leaving Canyon High School and running the same offense and defense at two other programs. He would win more championships. At St. Margaret's High School, Coach Welch won three CIF Championships and one state championship. He moved on to Santa Margarita High School, winning one CIF Championship and one State Championship, before ultimately retiring from coaching in 2013.

COACH KEVIN ROONEY, HEAD COACH, NOTRE DAME HIGH SCHOOL, SHERMAN OAKS, CALIFORNIA

Following the 2002 season, I returned to coaching at the high school level. I reached out to Coach Rooney, the legendary head football coach at Notre Dame High School in Sherman Oaks, California. I had known Coach Rooney for years (while at Muir, we had played and lost to his team in the CIF Semi-Finals in 1996) and always admired him from afar. There was always something about his demeanor of quiet intensity that intrigued me. When I met with him, I stressed to him I was just looking for an opportunity to learn from him and coach wherever he needed me. For the winter and spring of 2003, I attended all the coaches' meetings and worked with the outside linebackers once we began spring practice. When spring practice was over, I had learned a lot working with the program. However, I had a philosophical problem teaching at one high school (Canyon High School) and coaching at another. As much as I enjoyed the time I had with the staff, I felt it would be best to resign from my position, but the few lessons I learned in that short period proved invaluable.

The first thing I learned from Coach Rooney happened in those off-season coaches' meetings I attended. From day one, we broke down a list of things that had transpired on all three levels, from the positives to areas of improvement. I found this fascinating. In all the years I had been an assistant coach, we had never done that on any staff I was on. Since I was not part of the staff for the previous season, all the information that was shared was new to me. I listened as each coach explained all the positive things that had taken place over the course of the season. Many of the ideas shared were things I would never have thought of. Team chemistry, overcoming adversity, beating a rival, and many other positives were a source of pride that each level experienced. We then went over areas of improvement. This was the area of greatest interest to me, as I wanted to be a part of the solutions to improve the program. It amazed me that Coach Rooney served as more of a moderator for the meetings. Each coach for each level shared ideas and suggestions on how each team could improve. They did this while contributing ideas on how the program could improve overall. It was refreshing to see a head coach actually listen to and implement ideas that his staff was giving. I would take this exercise and use it in the future with my coaching staff.

The second thing I learned in that short time was the value of coaching everyone, regardless of talent or skill level. When we began coaching that spring, he and I coached the outside linebackers together. As I observed and assisted him, I watched him treat every player the same, regardless of whether the player was a returning All-League player or a first-year player on varsity. He coached each player the same.

All-League player or a first-year player on varsity, he coached each player the same. I realized there were some kids more talented than others, but to him, they deserved to be treated and coached with the same enthusiasm. This was a radical new concept to me. In the past, I was guilty of focusing on the players who I thought were going to be the major contributors while not paying much attention to the others. What stood out to me the most was that this was the head coach of a very successful program doing it. To him, it didn't matter. Each player was important, and his actions clearly showed that.

This was a valuable lesson for me to witness and carry with me in my future of coaching.

COACH JIM KUNAU, HEAD COACH, ORANGE LUTHERAN HIGH SCHOOL, ORANGE, CALIFORNIA

The final mentor that I'd like to share about was Coach Kunau. He was the head football coach at Orange Lutheran High School for 19 seasons, dating back to the early '90s. When I met with Coach Kunau following my second season as head coach of Saugus High School in 2004, it was a critical time in my coaching career. We had experienced some very challenging events that season and I was looking for some direction to improve our program. When I met with him, I was considering stepping down as the head coach. For reasons I will go into later in this book, I expressed to him my concerns. He asked me a very simple question when we started, "What is your vision for Saugus football?" I remember sitting there for a long time, and the best I could come up with was winning our league and a CIF championship. I was ashamed that this was all I could come up with. For the next several hours, we talked and went over various ideas and concepts that, for me, were brand new. Vision, mission, and core values dominated our talk. He gave me several books to read while recommending others I should explore upon leaving. I walked away from that meeting highly encouraged and will forever be in debt to Coach Kunau for taking the time to invest in me. I will discuss in more detail what specifically I learned and how I applied it to our program later in the book. For now, the best thing I got from Coach Kuanu was to take the time to invest in others.

SUMMARY OF MENTORS

While there are no doubt others who have been highly influential in my life, the people I have shared about are the ones who left the biggest impression on me. It blessed me to witness, observe, and take part in many of them. While this is not a complete list, it represents some major concepts that I could use for years to come. I will reference other things I learned from some of these individuals and others in later chapters.

2

13-YEAR ASSISTANT COACH: LESSONS LEARNED FROM THE TRENCHES

"It's what you learn after you know it all that counts."

—JOHN WOODEN

LEARNING AND GROWING: KNOW YOUR CRAFT

Once I made coaching football my chosen profession, I dove headfirst into learning as much as I could. I began reading many books on football. I enjoyed books on schemes and techniques. Others focused on building a program and philosophy, biographies, and stories of individual players, coaches, and teams. I also began reading as many books on leadership and management as I could. I would take the lessons applied to business and make them applicable to coaching football. One of the powerful practices I began early on was annotating the books I read. It was impossible to read without having a pen or highlighter to mark out ideas or concepts that I thought were important. Once I finished reading a book, I made it a habit of transcribing all my annotations into notebooks that I would fill up only to start a new one. This was the pre-computer days of the early 1990s. I'd like to say that once computers became more prevalent, I would type them in. I guess I'm old-fashioned because I still handwrite all my annotations in a notebook to this day. This practice has helped me tremendously as a coach, as it allowed me to track my growth and have a resource to reference.

Another practice I used to grow as an assistant coach was to attend coaches' clinics. Clinics were invaluable in that they exposed me to all kinds of information related to football. While in attendance, I would attack the clinic list of speakers and topics with intensity, focusing on concepts that I felt would make me a better coach. I would often sit in the very front so that I could stay focused, notebook and pen in hand, writing everything I could. Asking questions of the speaker did not bother me, regardless of who it was. I focused on ensuring I understood what the speaker was saying. It was at these clinics, especially in the early years of my career, that I would build a network of coaches willing to share their material with me. I was not above asking coaches for their contact information so that I could talk to them whenever I had questions. Finally, I kept all my notes in spiral-bound notebooks so that I had references over the years. These have been valuable resources that I have used.

Once I started coaching, I began reaching out to both high school and college coaches to see if I could visit their programs. This proved to be highly beneficial in seeing firsthand what other coaches were doing. Upon arriving on campus, regardless of a high school or college, I would sit with the coaches and grill them on anything I wanted to learn about. I had no issues asking coaches for information, regardless of what it was. I wanted to know everything they did so that I could either use it verbatim or change it to serve our needs. Learning from people who are very good at what they do seemed like a simple decision to me. Why wouldn't you want to do this? If you want to be great at what you do, learn from people who have come before you, take what they have done, and apply it to what you do. It just makes sense.

As part of the learning and growing process, I began collecting VHS cassettes of everything related to football. I would record games on TV and re-watch them, trying to learn what other teams were doing. As part of Coach Williams's FCPGA (see Chapter 1), I built a very impressive library of clinic films I would use to grow my knowledge. I would also purchase cassettes from the variety of vendors available to add to my library. When DVDs replaced VHS tapes, I began collecting those as well. All of this was invaluable not only to me but also to other coaches I would work with on staff as I shared all of this with them.

Another practice I began as a junior assistant was purchasing a daily planner to track all my activities. I would buy the kind a doctor's office would use, which had 15-minute time increments starting at 7:00 am to 8:00 pm to write in everything I was going to do throughout the day. This would benefit my professional and personal life. It allowed me to see where I was spending most of my time and allowed me to see where I could improve my time management skills. I still have all my daily planners that I refer to to this day.

Finally, if you want to be great, you must be obsessed with learning and growing. I heard Craig Bohl, the head football coach at the

University of Wyoming, say in a clinic, "You are either green and growing or ripe and dying." This really resonated with me. It clearly shows that if you want to be the best at what you do, you must put your ego in check. Make humility a huge part of your DNA, accept that you don't know it all, and be an active learner in personal growth. It's the only way I know how to get better.

LOYALTY

One of the first lessons I learned as an assistant coach was loyalty. This means you stay committed to your head coach and support him, regardless of what you believe. When you get hired to work for someone, they are putting their trust in you. They saw something in you that made them feel confident to hire you, so the least you can do while on their staff is to remain loyal.

There are many ways you can show your loyalty to your head coach. First, you need to take care of doing your assigned job. Regardless of the responsibilities given to you, it's on you to ensure the job gets done without the head coach having to ask if you got it done. This goes a long way in making the head coach feel he doesn't need to worry about the area you have. This may also lead to you being given more responsibilities.

Second, you support your head coach with the other assistants on the staff by speaking the same language the head coach speaks. This means that if you have concerns or disagreements, you either keep them to yourself or talk to the head coach directly in private. Many coaching staffs fell apart when assistants began talking negatively amongst themselves. This is especially true about things they disagree with that the head coach is or isn't doing. This creates a very toxic environment and does nothing but undermine the ability of the head coach to do what they are trying to do.

Third, you need to ensure you fully understand the expectations the head coach has for doing everything related to the team and program. You do this by asking the head coach for clarification anytime you are unsure. Once you understand what the head coach wants to be done, you carry it out to the letter. Yes, sometimes taking the initiative is a good thing, but you need to ensure that whatever it is you're doing is in alignment with their goals and expectations. There is nothing more damaging to a head coach than an assistant who has done things on their own without the head coach's knowledge. Or even worse, has done something that is not in alignment with their program expectations.

Fourth, you show your loyalty by keeping any concerns or disagreements you may have with the head coach out of the community. This means you are not talking to parents, administrators, or friends of yours in the coaching community. You never know who is going to talk to whom, and the last thing you want to happen is for something you said to someone outside the program to get back to your head coach. It is paramount that you always keep things "in-house" and go directly to the head coach. Doing anything else would be very damaging to you and any future you may have in the program you're in or any program you may go to in the future.

Finally, you must make a commitment to give the program and the head coach your undivided attention for the time you are working on the staff. This means that while on staff, the only thing that matters is carrying out the vision of the head coach to the fullest. You do everything in your power to improve your position group or unit within the confines of your head coach's expectations. I really embraced this concept. Frosty Westering's book, *Make the Big Time Where You Are*, really expressed this idea. He was the former head coach at Pacific Lutheran University in Washington. In his book, he talked about being present and where you are as the keys to success and happiness. If you're always looking for that next opportunity, you will never fully commit to where you're at and will thus not perform to your full potential. Sure, there will be times when other opportunities may present themselves. Job offers while you're working with your current staff may happen. However, you need to ensure that you finish the commitment you made with focus, vigor, and genuine effort. Once the season is over, you let your head coach know that you have been presented with another opportunity. You do this so that there is no perception of your head coach that it distracted you while working for him. They need to know that you have a commitment to helping them succeed despite getting offered another opportunity.

While this list is not absolute, these are the things that I learned as an assistant to the various coaches I worked with. Some or all of them may be a challenge, but they are necessary components of being a loyal assistant.

WORK HARD

While this idea is true in any endeavor, it is especially important in the coaching profession. You must do whatever it takes to get the job done, which may require making personal sacrifices. This could mean many things. Low pay, giving up time with family and friends, working on the weekends, getting up early, going to bed late, and many others. These need to be tempered by balance (will be discussed in a later chapter). It is critical that to be successful, you will need to outwork everyone else who is doing the same thing you are. Outworking others does not mean working longer, but it means that you will have to dedicate your time to get your work done. How you do this entirely depends on your situation.

I liked to get my work done early in the morning. This was when I was usually the sharpest and focused before the happenings of the day clouded my head. Watching films of opponents, creating drills for my players, working on scouting reports, and much more off-the-field work, I would do these as the first part of my day. Yes, sometimes more time is appropriate to get some of these things done, and it was up to my creativity to figure out when to do it.

Another area that you need to work hard in is on the field with the players. It may sound trivial, but it starts with your attire. I always ensured that I was wearing athletic clothing (usually provided by the program, but not always) and either tennis shoes or cleats. I needed to move and show the skills or techniques that my players needed to execute to be successful. Another critical thing is that you should not have sunflower seeds, food, or anything else that may distract you from coaching. This includes cell phones. While I understand the importance of us staying connected and having our phones, someone should only view it when needed. When you're on the field, your focus and energy needs to be directed on the players. They deserve our attention, and this requires hard work.

We need to coach with enthusiasm and energy and give players constant feedback. This, if done right, takes a lot of work and leaves you exhausted by the end of practice. If you want your players to be great, you need to give them all of you, and that requires hard work.

DO ALL THE THINGS NO ONE ELSE WANTS TO DO

What so many people don't understand about coaching football is the number of things that need to happen off and away from the field. Many of them have nothing to do with working with the players directly. 80% of a coach's job happens before the players step on the field. The work is in the details that never seem to end in preparing for practice and games. As an assistant coach, you need to do all the things that no one else likes to do, both compared to other programs and your own.

The head coach has a ton of things that need to be done that take him away from focusing on the strategic picture of the program and team. Often, he will make a list of things that need to be done and ask his assistants to take care of them. Your job as an assistant coach is to take ownership of the things the head coach has given you and do them above and beyond what they have asked. Not only do you need to do a great job of doing what you're tasked with, but you need to ensure that the head coach never needs to remind you of it. Take it off his plate and make him feel you've got him covered.

Besides what you're tasked with, do the things that need to be done without being asked. This could mean a variety of things. Take care of the water bottles and fill them up before practice. Putting air in the footballs when low. Setting up drill stations that the head coach may run. Ensuring that the cameras are up for practice and games. Fixing players' equipment. There are a variety of other tasks that nobody likes to do. By doing this, you show you are not above doing all the mundane tasks that often fall by the wayside and need to be taken care of. This shows your head coach that you are there to make his life easier and you care about the things that need to be done to ensure practice and games run smoothly.

BE ONE STEP AHEAD OF THE HEAD COACH.

While this concept sounds a lot like doing the things that no one else wants to do, it's a little more in-depth than that. This idea of being one step ahead of the head coach requires tremendous observation and listening skills. As an assistant coach, anticipate what the head coach needs to do to make his job easier. It requires you to be observant and always hunt out ways to ensure that the head coach can do the job he needs to do.

There are a variety of ways an assistant coach can do this. For me, I looked for ways to help the head coach by listening to him speak in meetings, during practice, or in games. If he mentioned something that was bothering him, regardless of what it was, I looked for solutions that might address the problem. It requires you to be in tune with the head coach and have a good understanding of what is important to him. It also requires you to be selfless and do the things that need to be done while not expecting any kind of recognition. The more you do, the more the head coach will notice and entrust you with more, and if he doesn't, don't worry; it will pay off in the long run. Trust me, if you do enough of this, it won't go unnoticed.

POSITION SPECIFIC ROLL CALL AND DRILLS

As an assistant coach, it is critical that you have your position group completely squared away. It is your job to ensure the players under your care know and do their job. A major part of that is ensuring you have a position roll call and drills created to ensure that your players are prepared to be successful.

A position roll call is simply a list of mental qualities, physical characteristics, and fundamentals a player needs to be great at his position. Your job as an assistant coach, in alignment with the head coach or coordinator, is to create this list for your players. You want to ensure that the players know exactly what they need to do to be successful.

This also allows them to know where they stand in the pecking order of other players by establishing a standard that determines who gets on the field. By doing this, you remove all doubt in the players' minds.

Drills are very important to a player's success. It's important to understand the difference between the drills used for each position. The two categories are basic position drills and scheme-specific drills. Basic position-specific drills are ones that focus on the technique and fundamentals a player will use in most plays. These drills are often called EDDs (every day drills) and are the backbone for playing the position. It is critical that the assistant coach knows how to teach and implement these techniques and fundamentals. Drills need to replicate what the player will need to do on a play-to-play basis. Some drills need to focus on building muscle memory, while others need to incorporate decision-making based on visual cues. Doing movement-only drills will not effectively train your players for game-like situations. You need to add visual cues. The players must react according to what they see while executing the fundamentals, which will make the players more prepared for the games.

Scheme drills are ones that require specific skills needed for play calls. These drills incorporate basic position-specific techniques infused into movements, stimuli, and responses. They relate to a play call. We typically introduce these drills in spring or summer and work on them periodically over the course of a season. If you're going to be running a specific play or scheme for that week, you would want to incorporate these drills with more frequency.

Another important aspect to understand is that doing drills for the sake of doing drills is a waste of time. If you're doing drills and not seeing them show up on game film, they need to be thrown out. Sometimes, we find the need to have an abundance of drills so that we keep our players busy and give the head coach the perception that we are working hard. Doing drills that focus on the movements, reads, reactions, and the finish of the fundamentals and technique is all that we need to improve our players.

When doing drills, there are several other components of drill work to consider. The first involves repetition. Drills need to be done repeatedly to ensure that they learn the movement pattern. They become a part of the player's natural reaction to the stimuli presented. When drilling in this manner, the players will become complacent while doing the drills because it becomes repetitive. Boredom can set in, which leads to lazy effort. As an assistant coach, you need to be diligent and enforce the maximum effort your players give to ensure the techniques being worked on do not degrade. This can be very exhaustive as a coach, but it must be done. This also involves giving constant feedback on each rep that the players execute. Any feedback you give must focus on what they are doing right, as well as what needs to be corrected. It's important to balance the two. Too much positive feedback may give the player the impression that there is nothing to improve upon. Too much correction may discourage the player from having confidence that they can do what you are asking of them.

The second involves employing a variety of drills to prevent complacency and boredom from the players. It may be challenging to create a variety of drills for certain fundamentals and techniques. It is imperative to try your best to create drills that are different but still work on the skills needed by the players. Sometimes, it only takes a subtle change to give the players the perception that it's a different drill while working on the same thing. This may involve using cones, agile bags, or trash cans. It could mean incorporating a ball or other props or any other way to make your drills different, but still work on the techniques the players need.

The third concept to employ is the use of doing drill work in mass. You want multiple players doing the same movements simultaneously as much as possible. We, as coaches, are constantly fighting the battle of time. You must try your best to do drills that require as many players as possible to ensure they are getting as many reps as possible. While this is not possible for all your drills, you want to limit the drills that focus on one player or a few players at a time. If this is not possible with certain drills, be sure to rotate the players through the drill in a fast, efficient manner. This ensures that players are getting as close to equal time working on the skills as possible.

The fourth idea involves direct instruction and commands when conducting drills. It is best to go over drills beforehand in a meeting. If you can't do this due to time restrictions, you need to ensure that you use as few words as possible when explaining a drill on the field. Time is valuable, and any drill that takes longer than 30 seconds to explain and execute is too long. Keep it short, focusing on how and why they are doing the drill, and get the players moving. You need to be aware of your body position when speaking to the players. Often, we get caught up in speaking to the players and don't realize that they can't hear us. You need to ensure everyone hears your voice, so position yourself in such a way that they can all hear your instructions. When starting or ending a drill, be cognizant of your use of a whistle. Remember, on defense, all plays start on a movement, not a whistle or verbal command. Try to implement this practice to the best of your ability when doing any defensive drill. You don't want your defensive players getting used to verbal cues when starting a play, so don't do it when doing drill work. For offensive drills, it's OK to use a verbal command (unless you're doing wide receiver drills; they should look at the ball) to start the movement. Finally, the use of the whistle should only end a drill. It sounds silly to even mention it, but you need to blow the whistle hard so that everyone hears it. That's how it's going to be done in a game, so ensure that you're only using a whistle to end a drill.

The final concept involves player-to-player feedback. Players giving each other feedback while doing drill work can be an effective way for players to learn. This serves several purposes. It gives the player giving the advice an opportunity to be a leader and ensures that they are paying attention to others. It allows the players to receive feedback from another set of eyes and coaching. This will help them improve and develop unit cohesiveness and camaraderie. Player-to-player feedback has always been one aspect of coaching a position I have encouraged among the players I coached.

COORDINATOR DUTIES

If you're a coordinator, you will have additional responsibilities on top of preparing your position players. It begins with having a philosophy that is in alignment with the head coach. Working with him, you will need to craft a plan of action on what your scheme will be and the goals you will have for the unit. You will then determine which players will be a part of that unit. This may be based on your head coach's philosophy of using a one or two-platoon system. I have worked with head coaches who firmly believed in having 11 players on offense and 11 players on defense. There have been other head coaches who believed in using the 11 best players (i.e., two-way players). Whichever is used, you will need to determine who those players will be. You will then need to determine what plays or calls you will use as the base of your unit.

One of the many things I learned from the head coaches I worked for was the idea of simplicity in terms of rules with whatever your base scheme was going to be.

Regardless of offense or defense, you will need to create very simple rules for the players to remember and follow to ensure they play fast.

The last thing you want is your players hesitating when you call a play. You want them to play with confidence by keeping things very simple. This also includes adjustments that need to be made once you have called a play. You want to keep adjustments to a minimum so that the players are executing with confidence instead of playing with hesitation.

Often, we as coaches think more is better in terms of the size of your playbook, but this can degrade your unit's effectiveness. You only have so much time to practice. If you have an abundance of calls, plays, and concepts, they limit you to how much time you can work on them to achieve some level of mastery. As a young coordinator, I was guilty of having too many calls in our playbook that I tried to run over the course of a season. I felt like the more I had the better prepared we would be for whatever the opponent threw at us. There is some merit in having answers for anything that your opponent uses against you. You also have the concept of your players getting overwhelmed, confused, and playing slow because they are thinking too much. There is nothing wrong with having a thick playbook filled with a variety of calls that you can employ. The trick is assessing your players and determining what you will use for a season based on the players you have. Some years, you may feel that you have a tremendous core of receivers and a quarterback, so using more passing plays may be prudent. Or, you have more defensive backs who prefer playing man coverage, so you use more blitzing. Whatever the case may be, you will need to adjust your playbook installation for the season based on what you have to work with.

Over the years, I forced myself to cut down on the number of calls in our playbook. I did this so our players could really focus on what our base calls would be. It is more effective to know a few concepts, plays, and calls extremely well versus having a bunch of stuff that the players only marginally know. Again, this is difficult. We, as coaches, get lured into believing that scheme wins when it is technique, fundamentals, and execution that leads to success.

Finally, there is nothing wrong with putting in a new concept that will be effective for an opponent. I have done this several times over the course of my career, but there are a couple of things to consider when doing this.

First, you need to ensure that whatever you are doing is not completely different from the concepts you already have in place. It should be a slight variation of concepts your players are already familiar with. This ensures that the players do not become confused or lose confidence that what they do as a normal part of your system is not good enough.

Second, you need to be prepared for mistakes that the players may make when putting something new in. As with any new play or concept being used, your players may not be 100% confident in using it and, thus, may make mistakes.

Last, you need to be prepared to ditch the concept if it is not working. Too many times, we get tunnel vision, believing that our idea should work and if we just give it time, it eventually will. You must put your ego aside and accept that the plan you had to employ something new is not working and go back to what you and your players know best.

Once your base scheme has been determined, you will need to create an installation plan. We typically do this over spring and summer practice leading up to fall camp.

There are two philosophies for installing during spring. One is to start with the most basic things you do and build upon those. While doing this, you're not moving forward until you feel confident that the players have grasped all the nuances of each call. This means that you continue to build and install over the rest of spring and summer. The other is introducing everything you plan on doing during the spring and then reviewing it over the summer. We have done both, each having its merits and drawbacks. Whichever you decide, stick to the plan and execute it.

Next, you will then need to drill it in a part-part-whole manner. Using group periods (inside run, seven on seven, and other various periods) and team periods, you work on the various components of your unit. One aspect of team football is situational periods (goal line, short yardage, 3rd down, Red Zone, blitzing/blitz pickup). Bill Walsh's book, *Finding the Winning Edge*, is a great resource to use to study the various situational aspects of football. The best way to manage this is to break it up over a week so that they are all covered. We would use the Thursday before game day to cover quite a few of them.

Once you are confident that you have adequately prepared your players over spring, summer, and fall camp, you will then transition into game prep mode. You will need to scout your up-and-coming opponents' film and begin tagging the film. When I first started coaching, we used VHS cassettes to review films. Later, these would transition into DVDs. Ultimately, online video, like HUDL, would replace all forms of video study. Handwriting all our notes on paper, compiling the data, and creating a scouting report on what the opponent was trying to do became essential. This was a very tedious but necessary process to understand what your opponent was trying to accomplish.

As time went on, using computers for both compiling data and watching films became more prevalent and time-efficient. Most coaches will use the last three games of an opponent to compile a general picture of their identity. They will identify their best players. What their top offensive plays/defensive fronts and coverages are, how they conduct themselves before/during/after each play, and studying their special teams. As a defensive coordinator studying a team's offense, I would watch every game on the opponent I could. I felt that three games were not enough for me to get a sense of what they were trying to do. Of course, the number of games they have played before you play them limits you, but if a team had played 4, 5, or 6 games before us, I was going to watch all of them. It gave me a sense of peace knowing I had seen all that they had done up to playing us. Finally, I would create a scouting report for our players. Truth be told, the report was more for me than the players, but I made copies for them, anyway. I would transition to giving the players digital scouting reports via HUDL to save time in copying and not stressing about whether players lost them.

With all the data collected, I would then create a game plan for the opponent based on the scouting report we created. This would involve collaboration with the other assistant coaches and the head coach. We would discuss what we really liked. We would then construct the practice plan for the week to reflect on what we thought was the best approach for addressing what the data had shown us. As the week progressed, we would always start with more than we probably needed and whittle it down as the week moved closer to game day. This practice served us well. If the players were having a difficult time executing a particular concept, we threw it out. We found that doing this lessened the pressure the players felt to perform. By game day, I had created the final call sheet for the game.

Once game day was upon us, we would remind the players of key coaching points that needed to be done for us to be successful. Once the game started, we would adjust as needed. This requires every coach to agree and see the same thing as the game progresses. By halftime, we would adjust and remind the players to stick to the plan and execute their fundamentals and techniques based on the calls. Win, lose, or draw, we would come in the next day, review the film as a staff, and make notes of positive aspects of the game and areas of improvement.

We would then bring the players in and review this information with them. We would then repeat the process all over for the next opponent.

As you can see, being a coordinator is a very taxing and all-encompassing job. The concepts I have listed are the major ones that were necessary for us to be successful as a unit and team.

MOVING UP AND/OR MOVING ON

When seeking a promotion, there are several ideas to consider while you're working in your current position. As mentioned earlier, it is critical that you stay focused on your current assignment. There are things you can do to prepare yourself for advancement, either within the current program or another one.

Regardless of the level you're working at and the position you're seeking, continue to give your current role your best effort. This is by far the most important aspect of seeking upward mobility, as it shows your commitment to the team and program. Once the season is over, the head coach will debrief his assistants regarding the season. The topics range from what just transpired to intentions to coach in the future. If working for a head coach who does not do this practice, seek a meeting with him as soon as he can meet. Once you meet with him, it is at this point that you let the head coach know your desires. It may be to move up from one level to another, change a position to coach or become a coordinator. Be very clear and specific about what you want to do in the program. Often, assistant coaches lose opportunities because they don't inform the head coach about their desired roles in the program. This puts the head coach on notice that you want to advance in your role on the staff. This does not guarantee you will get what you want, but at least you have informed him of your intentions. Usually, the head coach will give you an idea of when he can make a final decision on your request, but if he doesn't, simply ask when you can expect to hear from him.

Along with letting the head coach know of your desire to advance, you will need to exercise patience as you wait for your opportunity. In today's world, instant gratification has become the norm rather than the exception. A lot of junior assistants grow impatient nowadays, almost expecting to be given either a varsity position or a coordinator role.

There is a process. Some feel we should give it without earning it and/or going through the steps to become a brilliant assistant. There is something to be said for working your way up the ranks, building your skill set, and learning the variety of aspects coaching encompasses. If your focus is on titles and notoriety without going through the stages it takes to become a great assistant coach, you're in the business for the wrong reasons.

There are a lot of factors weighing on the head coach's mind when deciding regarding your request, and sometimes, this involves other coaches on his staff. Be patient and wait to hear from him. This can be a challenge, especially if you have been offered another position on a different staff. Navigate this with caution. You don't want to give your head coach the idea that you are trying to leverage that into getting what you want. Be open, honest, and upfront, but never try to back the head coach into a corner unless you are prepared to move on. If the head coach approves your request, then you should start working on improving and preparing yourself for your new role as soon as possible. If the head coach cannot grant your request, speak to him candidly and ask why.

Be prepared for an honest conversation. It may be something as simple as him not having the opportunity you're seeking. This may be because all the other coaches are returning, and he's not planning on moving anyone on the staff around. Or it may be because he doesn't feel you're ready to fill the position you're requesting. Whatever the case may be, be professional. Thank him for taking the time to consider your request, ask him what you can do to improve your chances for next season, and take some time to think about your options. You only have two options: remain in the same role for next season or seek another opportunity on a different staff. If you decide to stay on the staff, try as much as possible to be the best at what you do. When the conversation happens next season, it will be very difficult for the head coach not to promote you.

Another thing to consider is that while he may not grant your request at the time of the meeting, things can change over the course of the off-season. You never know if another coach on the staff may continue coaching, and if they leave, this may pave the way for your advancement. If you decide to explore other options, do so with caution and tact. You have every right to look for another position, but keep in mind that the head coach has every right to replace you as well. So, tread lightly when seeking another position. Always maintain a level of professionalism with your current head coach. If you get an interview with another staff, you'll want your head coach to give you a glowing recommendation.

Finally, if you decide to leave, regardless of whether you have another opportunity to coach somewhere else or not, always inform your head coach. Be sure to thank him for the opportunity to work on the staff and maintain a positive attitude as you depart. You don't want to burn any bridges. You never know if you're going to cross paths with this head coach again or need a recommendation from him should a future opportunity arise.

If you desire to be a head coach, let the head coach know as soon as possible. Most head football coaches want to help you in your desire to become a head coach, as they have gone through the same thing.

The best recommendation you can get for a new job you're applying for comes from your head coach. Make sure you do everything in your power to be the best assistant coach you can be. While you're waiting for job opportunities to open, begin compiling a list of ideas that will form your program philosophy.

The best way to do this is to keep a running log of things you want for your future program. These ideas come from the books you read, the clinics you attend, the coaches you speak with, and your own observations from your current program. Once you have begun this process, prepare your resume and a program manual for any future interviews that you may go on.

This manual should comprise your overall program philosophy. Be sure to include your offensive/defensive/special team schemes and weight training philosophies as well. It should also have a year one, year three, and year five plan (or any other number you see fit) on how you're planning on building and growing the program. Other things to put in this manual would include your academic plan for success for the student-athletes.

Address your plan for sharing athletes with other sports programs. Explain how your booster club will operate. Describe your plan for fundraising. Share how your coaching staff is to be structured. Add anything else you think may be of importance. By having this manual prepared and ready, you will walk into any interview with these ideas organized and ready to present.

RESEARCH, APPLYING, AND INTERVIEWING FOR A HEAD COACHING POSITION

Once you have decided to apply for a head coaching position begin seeking schools that may be a good fit for you. The only way to do this is to do your homework. After I was an assistant for a few years, I began the interview process for head coaching jobs but did so without doing adequate research. I simply heard of an opening and applied because I thought I was ready. After several interviews at various schools, I realized several things. These were based on debriefings with the people I had interviewed and my own observations.

I learned that the school already had someone else in mind and that they asked me to interview to ensure that there were enough candidates. This didn't bother me because I looked at it like I was getting valuable experience doing interviews.

Sometimes, I did not get the job because I lacked experience, which didn't bother me because they were right. I did lack experience. Yet, in others, I walked away thinking I nailed the interview and yet still did not get the job. While this was disappointing, I can tell you that there were several jobs I did not get that I was glad I didn't. This was especially true once I saw what happened to the program after another candidate got the job. I continued to seek interviews but did so by doing more intensive research into the positions I was applying for.

I would look at a school's previous football history and determine what had transpired over the years. Were they a perpetually losing program? If so, why? Was it because they lacked resources? Did they have an administration that was not supportive? Was there another sport on their campus that was a priority? Did they have a student make-up that made getting kids to come out and play football a challenge? Was the socio-economic demographics of the area one in which playing football was not important? Another question to consider would be, had they been successful in years past only to fall on hard times? If so, why? Many of the same questions above could apply in this scenario as well. Or maybe the school is successful, and their head coach moved on/retired, and they are simply looking to replace him.

Whatever the case may be, you need to find out the answers to these questions to the best of your ability before you apply.

One way to do this is by reaching out to the local newspaper that covers that school and asking them about their take on the program. Another way would be to track down the former head coach or assistants and ask them. This can give you some valuable insight into the school's makeup. Speaking to coaches who have played against that program over the years and getting their insight may be useful. Finally, reaching out to anyone who may have some information on the school or program can produce solid information. These can be very useful in determining if you even want to seek an interview with them. Regardless of where you seek employment, no job is going to be perfect. Each one will have its own set of unique challenges, but it's up to you to see if you can overcome them and be successful in the position.

For me, there were several "deal-breakers" that would prevent me from seeking employment at a school. First, if I felt the school did not make athletics, let alone football, a critical part of the educational process for the students, I would not be interested. I knew how important playing high school sports was for me and my growth as a person. Any institution that did not feel the same way was not a place that I wanted to work at.

Second, the administration had to be supportive of football. This meant that they would do everything in their power to help me succeed. This could mean giving me a favorable teaching schedule so that I can earn a living. Their support could also take the form of committing to hiring qualified on-campus teachers to coach on staff. This is critical if you want to run and maintain a successful program. Walk-on coaches are essential to any staff, but having guys on campus is invaluable (I will talk more about assistant coaches in a later chapter). Along those same lines, having complete control over who I keep, hire, or remove on my coaching/support staff was vital. If the school was not willing to trust me in who I selected to work on my staff, then it was a school I was not interested in working at.

Finally, to a much lesser extent, a lack of adequate facilities or the unwillingness to improve on existing ones may have been a reason for me not to apply. While I understand that this may be beyond the school's control because of space or funding, I at least wanted the basics, like a practice field and weight room. If the school lacked these two necessities but had a solution to them, then I was all in. If not, and they offered no solution that could accommodate our need for them, then I most likely would not seek an interview. I am sure there are other reasons that you may feel would be "deal breakers," but for me, these were the biggest.

Once you have done your homework and are sure that you have a realistic chance of getting the position, the next step is the interview. I always made it a practice to wear a suit and tie when interviewing. It shocked me when I first started interviewing how many other candidates showed up in shorts and a t-shirt or jeans and a polo. I assumed, maybe falsely, that everyone seeking a new position would wear a suit and tie. I think you only get one shot to make a first impression, and to me, wearing a suit was a simple decision.

Most of the first interviews I went through were by committee. It usually comprised the principal and/or assistant principal in charge of athletics and the athletic director. Sometimes, a teacher, a parent of either a current or former player, a current assistant coach, a current player, and/or a booster club member were present.

Before the interview begins, they will introduce you to everyone in the room. Be sure to make eye contact with each of them and try to the best of your ability to remember who you have been introduced to.

Hand out your resumes and your program manual to everyone in the room so that they may peruse it before the actual interview begins.

The committee will give you a little background after introductions have been made. They may share some information about the school, the football program, and anything else they feel is important. Have a notepad and pen ready to write anything they say that may be of value to you. Once their questions begin, there are a couple of things to remember.

One always makes eye contact with the person asking the questions. Second, once they ask a question, be sure you completely hear and understand the question, and if you don't, don't be afraid to ask for clarification. Nothing is more frustrating than having a question asked of you that you did not answer correctly because you misunderstood. If you understood the question, be sure to say something like, "That's a great question," or "I am so glad you asked that question," before you answer the question. People like to feel like what they are asking is of importance, and this is a great way to show them you feel that way. If they ask a question that you really aren't sure how to answer or you just simply don't have an answer, tell them that. There is nothing wrong with not having an answer. It shows you are human and you don't have all the answers. "That's a brilliant question, and to be honest, I don't have an answer for you right now, but I will have one for you the next time I see you." Another solid response would be, "You know, I have never really thought about that, but I promise you, I will have an answer for you the next time I see you." Be sure to write the questions that you did not answer on your notepad. Sometimes, the answer will come to you before you finish the interview, and you might circle back to it. By responding this way and writing it down, you're showing your humility about not having all the answers. You are also showing sincerity by writing it down, intending to get an answer for them in the future. By far, the worst thing you can do is try to "fake your way" through a question. People see right through that, and usually, your response is not your true feelings or thoughts. Just be honest with them. People appreciate that.

Another thing to be prepared for is scenario questions. Most of the interviews I went on involved these types of questions. They almost always involve a question regarding an angry parent who's upset with their child's lack of playing time. Another popular one is a star player who has gotten into trouble at school and how you plan to deal with it. Some involve an opponent or official who has committed an error during a game. Still, another may involve a player who has disrespected or been defiant to a coach. These are all designed to reveal your method of dealing with challenging situations. I have always found it best to be honest when answering these types of questions. Don't be afraid to ask for clarification, and to take your time when answering. Really think it through because your answers may very well reveal your character to the people asking them.

Once they have completed their questions, they will usually ask if you have questions for them. It's now your turn to interview them. I always found this to be an especially helpful practice to gain a better understanding of what exactly they were looking for in their next head coach. I also felt that by asking them questions, I was not simply there just to get a job. I wanted to ensure that I was the right person for the job, and the best way to find that out was to ask them questions. Usually, my questions revolved around asking them what exactly they were looking for in terms of the next head coach. What are their expectations for the program? How do they see the head coach serving their needs? The answers to these questions can be very revealing and helpful in determining if this job is right for you. This also makes them feel you are genuinely interested in their school and program.

Finally, upon ending the interview process, thank each member for their time and let them know you look forward to hearing from them. If you get a callback for a second interview, expect to answer more questions from the interviewer. Follow your heart and answer them honestly. Sometimes, the second interview isn't an interview at all but a job offer. If you do not get a second interview or they inform you that you did not get the position, thank the person who called. Inquire about the person who called for the reason behind not being selected. Ask for suggestions on how to increase the probability of being selected next time.

SUMMARY OF LESSONS LEARNED

These are some lessons I learned over the course of 13 years as an assistant coach leading up to my first (and only) head coaching job. While there are many others, these were the ones that made the most lasting impact on me. If you take these lessons and apply them to your unique situation, you will be a success no matter what course of action you take.

3

1ST YEAR AS A HEAD COACH: WHAT WORKED, WHAT DIDN'T

"Discipline is getting better every day."

—TIM KIGHT

In July 2003, I interviewed for the head coaching position at Saugus High School in Santa Clarita, California. For some of you reading this, you may think, "July? Isn't that right before fall camp? Are you sure about this?!" You would be correct. I interviewed for a position five weeks before the start of fall camp. Let's back the story up a bit.

WINNING WITHOUT A CHAMPIONSHIP

Saugus was one of four high schools in the Santa Clarita Valley, about 40 minutes north of downtown Los Angeles. It is also home to the theme park Six Flags Magic Mountain. I was working as a teacher at Canyon High School, also in the Santa Clarita Valley and part of the same district as Saugus, when I interviewed for the position. Recently, I resigned from my assistant coaching position working with Coach Rooney at Notre Dame High School. I was talking with Coach Welch at Canyon about possibly returning to his staff for the 2003 season. When the Saugus High School head football coach resigned his position in late June, they officially flew the job the first week of July 2003.

Saugus had fallen on hard times. The program had competed in the tough Foothill League, which was comprised of Hart, Valencia, Canyon, Burbank, and Burroughs High Schools. But as of late, they had really struggled. When the position opened, there were few people beating the door down to become their next head coach. Why would they? You get to play in a highly competitive league. There is no luxury of spring or summer practice. You do not know what players you have, and you most likely will not have enough time to hire a full staff. For me, it was the perfect opportunity that could not have come at a better time.

For starters, the school had just hired a new principal, who had been an assistant principal at Canyon. I had worked with him for two years while at Canyon and really liked him. He had a background in sports, was a former coach and athletic director, and was extremely positive. Second, they had also hired a new athletic director. Talk about a perfect scenario. I was applying for a position that most people were not interested in, and the two people directly responsible for hiring the new head coach were brand new as well. This primed the school and program for a new direction. After applying, I received a call several days later to come in for an interview. Armed with all the knowledge I had gained up to this point in my career, I was ready for the challenge.

When I arrived for the interview dressed in a suit and tie, I entered the interview room with my resume and program manuals in hand. Greetings took place with everyone on the committee as I handed out my materials and began answering questions. I was prepared for each question they asked. I felt relaxed, confident, and encouraged by how the interview process was going. To the best of my recollection, I can't remember ever being stumped by any question that was asked of me. When they finished asking me questions, they gave me the opportunity to ask them questions, many of which were the same ones offered in the previous chapter. I left the interview feeling very confident that I had addressed all their concerns and that I was a good fit for their school. Several days later, I received a call to come back for a second interview, which is a complete blur today. I had been on second interviews before, but this one felt different. The questions being asked of me were more a formality than an interview. At the end of this interview, they officially offered me the position of head coach at the ripe old age of 32.

Once hired, they introduced me to the players, and I immediately began observing the last week of summer practice. The players were performing before going on their three-week dead period. I refrained from stepping in and coaching. I watched the players perform in the weight room and on the field as the remaining assistant coaches put them through the training. My initial thought was that we had an excellent group of kids who worked hard and needed some guidance. Once this week of practice was over, I began working with the coaches to ensure that we aligned our plan.

I began building a staff with the existing coaches and bringing in others. This was not a simple task. We were late into the summer, and most of the assistant coaches I wanted to bring on board had already committed to other programs. I decided to have one staff that would coach both the Varsity and JV teams and a separate staff that would coach the Frosh team. I made this decision for several reasons. One, we did not have enough coaches to fill out three complete staffs. Two, I wanted to ensure that all three levels were running the same system. And three, I barely knew any of the current staff members and needed to keep a close watch on what was being taught to ensure that it was being done the way I wanted. Several members of the JV staff elected to resign their positions because they did not want to be a part of the structure I was establishing. No matter how hard I tried to convince them, they simply decided not to continue coaching. I felt, that by organizing the staff this way, it was the fastest, easiest, and most efficient way to ensure that the program was in complete alignment. They, however, felt it was time for them to move on. I did not take it personally, as I understood that if you don't believe in what the head coach is doing, why stick around?

For the next few weeks before fall camp began, I met with the remaining staff and the few coaches I brought on board. We assigned roles and responsibilities. I began indoctrinating them on how I wanted things to be done. The staff shared their opinions on talent, strengths, and weaknesses and how to use the existing players. I shared with them my expectations of how to conduct themselves with both the players and parents. We discussed how I wanted the practices to be run, how the weight room was going to look, and what steps we needed to take before the players reported back to camp.

Finally, I informed the staff that I was going to call both the offense and defense. I would do this until I could give those responsibilities over to someone who I felt understood what I wanted to be done. Given the short time we had, I was confident that the pieces were in place for us to begin the campaign on a positive note.

Once the players reported back to camp, we began the process of instruction, installing our scheme and the fundamentals of the game. It became apparent rather quickly that while this group of young men were willing participants, many of them were not in shape and lacked some of the basic skills needed to perform. They needed a lot of guidance on how to play the various positions for the system we were putting in. Each day, our focus rarely strayed from the basics for each position and our scheme. We kept it very simple to ensure each player fully understood what we wanted from them. As we moved closer to our first contest, we had a couple of bumps in the road.

The week before our first game, one of the better players on the team quit. It caught us all by surprise, as he was doing extremely well. When I sat him down to discuss his reasons and rationale, he could not give me a clear-cut answer other than he simply lost interest. Once he left, I asked some of the other coaches what their take on his decision to quit was. They stated that the young man had a reputation for "partying." He was not willing to continue with the standards and expectations that we were establishing. This was my first introduction to what to expect from talented players who did not want to do things the way we wanted. As frustrating as it was, we had to let him go. I hoped that more players would not follow suit.

Another challenge we experienced was a rash of injuries. While common when playing the game of football, we had an unusual number of them leading up to our first game. I made the tough decision to pull back on the amount of contact we were engaged in during practice. I was still trying to access and gauge who could do what on our team, and having to limit our contact made this very difficult.

We would travel to San Diego, California, to play our first contest versus Hilltop High School. While long road trips were not new to me, this trip proved to be both challenging and exciting. We arrived on campus and began our pre-game preparation of getting dressed and heading out to the field. The game did not begin on a positive note as the opponent ran back the opening kick-off for a TD. Once we got over the initial shock, we settled down and played our brand of football. We would end up winning the game, but we had a long way to go. As the season progressed, we would only win one other pre-season contest and then lose all five of our league games, finishing the season with a 2-8 record. While it was a disappointing campaign on so many levels, I learned valuable lessons from the experience.

WHAT WORKED?

Combined staff

Once hired, I used a combined staff model. As mentioned earlier, I had one staff who coached the JV and Varsity teams, while a separate staff coached the Frosh level. For the combined staff, I had five defensive coaches and five offensive coaches. Each coach would work with their position group for one hour at one level, then switch and do the same with the other level. By doing this, each coach was coaching all the players in his position group for both the JV and Varsity. This was a very effective model in that each coach got to work for his position group twice a day, allowing them to get better at coaching. A varsity assistant was coaching the JV players, which would help prepare them for their Varsity season. I selected two assistants to serve as coordinators for the JV team. I served as the head coach for the team in title but did little on game day with them, as I was with the Varsity team. The only challenge to this system is that your assistant coaches will get taxed on game day, both physically and mentally. Regardless of what happened during the JV game, they had to flush it and be mentally ready for the varsity games. In terms of preparation for up-and-coming opponents on the JV level, we watched very little film and kept our game plan geared toward what we did. All our focus was on preparing for the Varsity game.

Learning to trust your assistants

As the season progressed, I realized some assistants were stronger than others and were clearly ready to be top-notch assistants. As stated earlier, I was calling both the offense and defense. But, I came to rely on the input of a few of the assistants more and more and handed over more responsibilities to them as the season progressed. This initially was difficult to do as I wanted to ensure we did things my way, not because of my ego or because my way was the only way, but it was the way I knew. If things went wrong, I knew what needed to be done to fix it. This also allowed me to take full responsibility for any shortcomings our team experienced. With each passing week, I trusted a few of the assistants with more, eventually handing over the defense to one of my assistants to finish out the season. Once I did this, there was a certain level of peace that came over me, as I could focus on other areas of our team that needed my attention.

Adjusting as needed when challenges arise

From the start of camp to the end of the year, we experienced a variety of challenges. Players were quitting. We had a rash of injuries. The realization that what we were trying to do schematically was not working. I learned to adjust and let go of certain things that I felt were no longer worth fighting for.

One challenge I previously mentioned was injuries. From camp all the way through the season, it seemed like players were dropping like flies. We adjusted our practice schedule to lessen full-contact drills, yet players were still getting injured. It's been a few years, but if memory serves me right, we had at least three players who blew their knees out and could not compete for the rest of the season. All three players were two-way players who also contributed to special teams. It was like losing nine players! We changed practice even more to take out contact completely.

Another change we made was to cross-train players to play multiple positions. This isn't anything revolutionary. We realized that with the injuries we had sustained, we needed to ensure that if another player got injured, we had developed others who had at least a little training and experience. This proved to be very beneficial in that players learned multiple positions, which made us better as a team and ready to adapt if needed.

As each week passed, we realized that some plays we were calling on both offense and defense were not working. There were a host of reasons as to why this was happening, all of which fell on me as the head coach—a change needed to be made. We adjusted the play-calling to ensure our players were in a better position to be successful. This meant making small tweaks to existing calls and/or completely omitting others. By doing this, we gave the players confidence that they were no longer being asked to do things they could not do. This also allowed coaches to really hone in and focus on a few things and get great at teaching, rather than a bunch of stuff that we were average at doing.

Adjusting as needed may seem like common sense, but sometimes we, as coaches, get stuck in our routine, ego, and mindset, unwilling to bend or change what we do. If what you're doing isn't working or worse, it's hurting your team, you need to adjust what you're doing.

Thursday team meals

One thing that we began doing was having a team meal at a player's home each week on the Thursday before our games. I got this idea from Coach Ladouceur from De La Salle High School.

Each week, we asked a family to volunteer their home for our team meal and other families to provide the meal. This was a great opportunity for the players to be away from school and work on their social skills. We made sure the players were polite, said please and thank you, and took care of the home we were in. It was also a great way for parents to contribute and feel like they were part of the program. We had no issues getting families to volunteer their homes or meals.

Once we finished eating and cleaning up, we would have a players and coaches-only meeting. This would either take place in the backyard, garage, or big room if the house had one. We would then hand out pens and 3x5 cards for the players to write their goals for the game the next day. Each player would scribble down things they wanted to accomplish during the game to help our team be successful. This included both starters and back-ups. We explained to the players that the goals they wrote needed to be **SMART** goals (specific, measurable, attainable, relevant, and time-bound). If on Saturday morning, after playing the game, you could not determine if you achieved your goals, we made them rewrite them. Once the players finished this, we had them choose a teammate. They would stand up, face each other, and share their team goals with each other, making a commitment to accomplishing the goals stated. We called these commitment cards. Once each player completed this task, we then allowed the players and coaches to give any last words regarding the game to be played the next day. This was a great way to wrap up the week and get everyone involved focused on the game.

Often, this became very emotional as players and coaches shared what was on their hearts and minds. It made the team very close and strengthened the bonds between everyone.

Scheduling pre-season games

While you have no control over who you play in your league, we needed to reevaluate our pre-season schedule. We had played some pretty tough teams and needed to make some adjustments that would allow us to compete while being challenged.

A philosophy that I embraced was the one win, one toss-up, and one challenge format. This meant scheduling a team we should beat, a team in which the game would be a toss-up game, and a team that would be very difficult to beat. Since our league comprised six teams, our five preseason games would have to comprise this formula plus two additional games. By having this format, we could better prepare our team for league play.

There are a couple of other things to consider when scheduling these preseason games. This includes scheduling teams that run a similar offense and/or defense to teams that you will face in either your league or your division in the playoffs. By doing this, you give your team valuable experience facing similar schemes that you will face in the future. I made it a point not to schedule teams that ran systems that would not benefit us. Sure, there is something to be said for playing teams that may not prepare you for future opponents, but I avoided doing this.

Another thing I did was schedule teams that were geographically close to us. Road trips offer unique challenges, but for me, traveling for more than an hour on a non-chartered bus (i.e., the big yellow bananas) was taxing on the players and coaches. Being cramped in a bus with all the players, coaches, and equipment for an extended period takes a toll on everyone. If we were going to travel for more than an hour, I chartered a coach bus. Some of these factors are unavoidable. I did everything I could to use the formula for scheduling opponents with all the above considerations.

Seeking counsel from mentors and others

As the season progressed, I made it a point to seek counsel from several sources, including some of my mentors, when faced with various challenges. They would provide support, suggestions, and answers to questions I had.

Humility is a noble quality to have, especially when you're a first-time head coach. No matter how much you try, you will not have all the answers. This is when you need to put your ego in check and not be afraid to seek help from others, especially people you trust who have gone through the same things you have. I made it a habit to reach out to several of my mentors during the season, asking for advice on how to best handle some challenges we were facing. This included off-the-field stuff like parental issues, players missing practice, and booster club concerns. Injuries, practice planning, and opponent scheming are among the other concerns on the field. Regardless of what the issue was, I rarely received advice that was not helpful. In the end, many of the people I reached out to wanted me and our program to be successful.

WHAT DIDN'T WORK?

Calling both the offense and defense

To ensure the implementation of what I wanted us to run, I called both the offense and defense when they hired me. While this may be true for any head coach, it proved to be very challenging for me on a multitude of levels.

The first issue to arise once the season progressed was the amount of work involved in managing both units. Each week, I would break down the opponent's defense and offense to prepare the game plan for the week. This took an enormous amount of time and energy. I justified calling both units initially because I did not know which assistants I could trust to run the unit. We were all still learning about each other, and my insecurity in handing over a unit to an assistant I hardly knew did not sit well with me.

The second issue in doing this was the level of exhaustion I felt. I was burning the candle at both ends, and by the time we got to game day, I was physically and mentally exhausted. My frayed nerves led me to make some poor choices in play calling during games. Other areas of my life were suffering as well (home life, academic duties, health), and I knew I could not keep up this pace.

The third issue with my lack of delegating one or both units to one or more of the assistants was the feeling of resentment I felt from some of the assistant coaches. In deciding to run and call both units, I knew some coaches were feeling alienated and that their opinions were not being respected. If I wanted to develop and keep any of these coaches for the next year, I knew I would have to give up at least one unit. Before the season ended, I turned over the defense to an assistant who I felt understood what we were trying to do, and he did an amazing job. He would end up serving as our defensive coordinator for the next few seasons.

Communicating expectations to assistants with little follow-up

In the weeks leading up to fall camp, I met with all the coaches and communicated my expectations on a variety of topics. In doing this, I expected the coaches to not only understand what I wanted but to execute what I had communicated. My expectation was simply this: do what I ask, how I asked when I want it done. Even typing these words makes me cringe. I would learn over the course of the season that this method does not work.

Over the course of my career as an assistant, I learned to listen intently to the head coach's expectations. I would frequently follow up to ensure I was doing what he wanted. My mistake was thinking that the assistants working with me would do the same thing without me having to remind them. This did not happen. Not only were my expectations not being met, but things were being done that were the opposite of what I had wanted. This, of course, was not the assistant coaches' fault, as I failed to remind and correct them consistently. Again, a lack of maturity on my part prevented me from doing this. As the season progressed, I grew more and more frustrated by the failure of some assistants to do what I wanted them to do. I would lose my temper and lash out, especially during meetings. This, of course, is no way to lead people, especially for ones who are coaching because they have a passion for working with young people, not to mention the fact that they are making little to no money for the time they are putting in. I failed to be a consistent and effective communicator of my expectations.

If you are going to be a head coach, you must be diligent in ensuring that what you want done is being done consistently in alignment with your expectations. The best way to ensure this is through observation and feedback, usually done before or during practice. If you see something during practice that is being done that you can't wait until after practice to correct, pull the coach aside from the players. I would usually do this during a water break and talk to him about what I would like to see done differently. When practice is over, meet with the coach privately and review why you talked with him so he has a better understanding of what you wanted. It also gives him a chance to express why he is doing what he is doing and allows for an open dialogue. Like in any relationship, open, frequent, and honest communication is critical for success.

Relying on a scheme that doesn't fit your players and league

When changing from an assistant to a head coaching position, you must decide on the type of offense and defense you are going to employ. You must commit to sticking with it as the season progresses. Your coaches and players need to commit and work hard to do it as well. One mistake I learned after that first season was using a scheme that did not fit well with our league. While sticking with your scheme, regardless of your opponents, you must consider the players you have. You must balance their ability to execute the scheme you're using with what you need to do to win games, especially in your league.

The Foothill League, which Saugus H.S. belongs to, was one in which passing the football was king. That's not to say that running the ball was not happening. But if you wanted to win games, you had to score points quickly and prevent teams who could do so, which in our league was being done by passing the ball. Hart, Valencia, and Canyon High School were the top teams in our league when I became the head coach. All three of them had highly explosive offenses that scored a lot of points by throwing the ball.

I had a run-dominant offense and a stout defense when I became the head coach. My philosophy was simple. If the opponent had less time on offense because our offense was eating up the clock, they would have fewer opportunities to score. There are some challenges to this thought process. What if they could score quickly using fewer plays and time off the clock, and your defense could not slow down or prevent their offense from scoring? It didn't matter how much time you ate up on the clock with your offense.

There were several games that season where we had the ball for large tracts of time and scored, only to give the ball back to them, and they scored quickly. Even worse, we ate up a bunch of time off the clock, didn't score, turned the ball over to them, and they scored. It became increasingly more difficult to score quickly when we relied so heavily on running the ball. Second, if you don't have a dominant offensive line and lack explosive running backs, it can make scoring that much more challenging.

Before our game began against Valencia High School that season, I had a conversation with Coach Brian Stiman, their head coach. I had been following his team over the years before I became the head coach at Saugus. I had watched them transition from a run-dominant offense to a more pass-oriented offense. When I asked him why he made that switch, his answer was very enlightening. Hart High School was the dominant team in the league, and they had done so with a prolific passing game. His team had a run-dominant offense, which they ran very well. Each year, they had trouble replicating Hart's passing attack in the week before they played them. The game would prove challenging for their defense because of this reason. He made the switch to a more pass-oriented offense that resembled Hart's offense. They did this so that his defensive players would work against it all spring, summer, and fall, leading up to their game against Hart. This, he felt, gave them a much better opportunity to compete and beat Hart. Not only did they prepare their defense better, but it also allowed their offense to score more points. They did this in a shorter time while throwing the ball using fewer plays. It made sense to me.

I opted for a more balanced approach on the offensive side of the ball. I didn't fully believe in the concept of passing the ball as much as some teams in our league did, but I committed to making changes. When we began our off-season research, we invested time in developing our pass attack that would complement our run game. We tried to create more play-action passes, quick set passes, screens, sprint-outs, and some longer developing pass plays. This would allow us the chance to score quickly in a shorter amount of time and improve our offensive unit so that we did not have to rely on our run game.

Finally, while developing our pass attack became a priority, it did not mean that I did not commit us to running the ball. We had several very talented players following the 2003 season that allowed us to rush the ball highly successfully. Adjust what you do to best fit the players you have as well as the league you're playing in.

Trying to be someone else

As a first-time head coach who studied a variety of coaches, I made the mistake of trying to be like some coaches I admired to where I was not being my natural self. I tried to do things I saw other teams and programs doing because I believed it would give us the best chance to be successful. This led me to do things that were not only out of character but also hurtful to our team.

One thing I tried to do was emulate De La Salle High School's vaunted split-back veer offense. While we were successful, we did not execute it to the level we needed to in order to dominate our opponents to the level they did. We lacked the talented players that they had. I also did not do an excellent job of teaching the coaches and players all the nuances needed to make the offense as good as it could be.

I also tried to be like Coach Ladouceur of De La Salle on the sidelines. After watching several of their games on TV and documentaries featuring his program, I tried to be very stoic, like Coach was in my observations. The issue is that I get very excited and intense, which is not like Coach Ladouceur's stoic demeanor. The more I tried to refrain from my emotions during games, the more difficult it became to control myself. I eventually learned that you must be you.

Another thing I did the first season was wear a short-sleeve shirt, sweater vest, and tie, just like Jim Tressel from Ohio State. I admired his demeanor and dress on game days, and so I wore the same thing. Again, I was trying to emulate someone else instead of being myself. It may sound trivial to clothing on game day, but as each week passed, I found myself physically uncomfortable wearing a tie on game day. While there is nothing wrong with coaches dressing this way, I found it to be very restrictive and ditched it after the season, replacing it with a polo and jacket.

As coaches, we naturally gravitate towards doing things like other successful coaches or programs do. Falsely, we believe we can do the same thing exactly as they do. We may try to be like someone we admire, again believing that this will make us a better coach. The problem with this is that you don't know all the facts, details, and work that goes into what other coaches or programs are doing to make them successful. There are a lot of factors, some of which we are not aware of, that go into what these programs are doing. While it is admirable to study what they do and how they do it and learn from the best, you must do what is best for your players and program while being yourself. You can take bits and pieces from different coaches and programs and infuse them into what you do. This is by far the best way to run your program and implement the things that you see others doing.

Not being actively involved in the booster club.

While there were booster clubs with the programs I had coached for as an assistant, my interactions with parents were extremely limited. Once I became the head coach, I had to navigate this extremely carefully.

The Saugus Gridiron Club was an established entity that had been used to doing things their own way.

One of the first obstacles I had to overcome was the petty bickering between various members of the executive board. There were some forceful personalities in leadership positions. They made sure that everyone knew what their opinions were while working behind the scenes to ensure their own personal agendas were being carried out. I did a lot of observing that first season, and the more I saw, the more I was determined to make some significant changes once the season was over. Where I failed was not asserting myself more during our meetings to ensure that we were all driving towards the same goal.

The number one purpose of any booster club is to support the head coach in whatever they need to run a successful program. Some members of our booster club did not agree with this concept and actively worked against me. Most of the time, it was subtle, but they were driven by what they wanted. This usually involved doing things that would directly benefit their own children while at the expense of others. Some members of the booster club felt that the head coach worked for the booster club instead of the other way around. There needed to be a major cultural shift in how things were being done, and I waited until the season was over to do this. In hindsight, I should have made the adjustments as the season progressed rather than waiting. It made making changes after the season that much more difficult. People continued to operate under the impression that I was OK with how things were being done.

Once the season was over, I immediately went to work restructuring how our booster club was going to work. What became clear to me was that our booster club was not a 501c3 organization. A 501c3 is a non-profit organization. It has its own bank account, its own tax ID number, a constitution that comprises by-laws, an elected executive board, and a set procedure on how to operate. We were the furthest thing from this.

We had our own bank account off campus that was not being run by the school's ASB (Associated Students Body), and we were using the school's tax ID to conduct business. The issue with this is a lack of oversight in terms of money. This can lead to irregularities in how the money is being spent and create a situation where embezzlement can take place. While there were no issues of this happening in the past or present time that I was aware of, this, as I was told, was how it had always been done. I consulted with some parents who were well-versed in running non-profits; we completed becoming our own 501c3 non-profit organization. It was my lack of understanding of how money was being collected and spent over that first season that really got me more involved in our booster club.

Another thing I did was help create our new constitution and bylaws. I did this to ensure that I had complete control over appointing who our president was going to be. This applied to our team representatives (commonly called team moms) as well. In the past, they elected these positions, which often became a popularity contest. I wanted to eliminate this because it had created tension between various sets of parents that first season. I did my research in terms of these positions and selected people whose mindset was in alignment with what I wanted to do with our program. Another important consideration in selecting these folks was to ensure that they had no hidden agendas. They needed to work in the best interest of all the players and families, regardless of who their child was in the program. While this can be much more difficult to root out, you must observe, listen, and ultimately go with your gut for selecting these individuals. So far, I have been truly blessed, after that first season, the number of issues we have had with our leadership and team representatives has been minimal.

Meetings, meetings, and more meetings

As a newly hired head coach, it was critical for me to get information communicated to the various groups connected to our program. While email is a great tool to use, sometimes meetings in person for different purposes, such as a dialogue between the people in attendance, is required. However, you must ensure that you don't spend too much time in meetings and neglect other priorities. You need to protect your time.

When hired as the head football coach, a teaching position accompanied it. This required that I attend school-related meetings, such as department meetings and full staff meetings. There was nothing I could do about these meetings, as I was contractually obligated to attend them. Most of our teacher-related meetings were after school, which meant missing a portion of practice, but I could manage these. It was the host of other meetings that really ate up my available time.

Because I wanted to make myself available to as many people as possible, I made the mistake of not managing my time effectively. Our player meetings took place at lunch, usually watching films, as well as watching a few more right before we headed out to the field. These meetings were essential, and there was no way around them. It was the other meetings after practice and on the weekends that I did not do an excellent job of managing.

I reserved weekends for film review with the players after our Friday night game and coaches' meetings. Once we reviewed the film with the players, we would dismiss them and begin preparing for the next opponent. This would usually take most of the day on Saturday, with homework assignments being distributed. We would then meet as staff on Sunday to create our game plan and a practice schedule for the week. Once completed, we would then head home, only to return on Monday for practice.

1st Year as a Head Coach: What Worked, What Didn't

I justified this schedule because we did not have enough time to do all we needed on Saturday, not to mention that fatigue would set in, and we needed a break. This was a very arduous routine as it meant we were doing football related activities seven days a week. The coaches were there with me each time we met, but I could tell as the season progressed, it was taking its toll on all of us. As the season drew near the end, I let the coaches know they could opt out of Sunday meetings. Some had already done this earlier in the season because of family commitments. This made it a little better for them, but I was still coming in to get the work done. Nowadays, with the digital video platform HUDL, game films are now online and accessible by all the coaches, 24 hours a day. This has allowed a coaching staff to do a much better job managing their time and workload.

Sometimes, during the week following a practice, we, as coaches, would need to meet. I did this to discuss changes that needed to be made based on observations from practice, a player injury, or some other reason. These meetings usually took place on the field and were much more informal. Sometimes, we would need to go to the classroom to go over stuff on the board, but this was rare. Other times, I would have to meet with a player following practice. While these meetings were much shorter in nature, they took up time.

Booster club meetings also happened during the week, usually once a month on Wednesdays. Sometimes, there would be two separate booster meetings in a week (one for the executive board and another comprising everyone else). I tried to attend all booster meetings during the season, which ate up another day that I couldn't be home.

Another activity that took place before I became the head coach was players, parents, and friends would meet at a local pizza restaurant on Tuesday nights. They did this to watch the game film from the previous Friday's game. It was a social gathering, which I thought was a great idea, but again, it was another night being taken away from me. I had already committed to team meals on Thursday nights, games on Friday nights, meetings on Saturday and Sunday, and a monthly booster club meeting. Adding one more night a week was too much. I decided not to attend these gatherings. Part of being a coach is learning how to balance all the factors pulling on you. It is critical that you maintain this to ensure that you're not devoting all your energy to one endeavor, which will eventually cost you in other areas. I will address this in more detail in a later chapter.

SUMMARY OF LESSONS LEARNED

My first year of being a head coach was one of the most exciting, challenging, and invaluable learning experiences of my life. Each week presented new opportunities to learn and grow. Some of those lessons were joyous, while others were painful, but I would not trade them for anything.

4

BUILDING A CULTURE: VISION, MISSION, CORE BELIEFS

"Vision without execution is hallucination."

—Thomas Edison

Culture. The word itself produces all kinds of thoughts and ideas in our society. In the arena of sports, it has been a huge buzzword over the past few years. Listen to any head coach of any sport, and you will often hear of the culture that drives their organization. Entire books are being written on the subject. Podcasts devoted to explaining what it looks like are happening daily. Clinic speakers have made it a major part of their talks. There are companies that exist to teach organizations how to develop, implement, and maintain their culture. My understanding of culture began with my meeting with Coach Kunau (refer to Chapter 1) back in 2004. That meeting set me on a course that has remained with me throughout my coaching career. For me, the idea of culture took years of fine-tuning to get to where we are today.

VISION: BE THE BEST VERSION OF YOU (YOUR WHAT)

"Better today than you were yesterday, better tomorrow than you were today."

To establish a culture, you must start with your vision, which asks, "What is it we want to accomplish in the work we do?" The idea of a vision is one that defines the "what" of your organization and where you want to go in the future. It is the driving force that enables you to stay focused on everything you do without deviation. When times get tough, and if you do anything long enough, they will, you need something to fall back on to get back on track. Vision allows you to do this.

Throughout our meeting, Coach Kunau would ask me a series of questions to stimulate my thoughts on what I wanted to accomplish with our program. The more we talked, the more I realized I saw one for our program but could not articulate it. Discouraged at first, Coach Kunau would share his thoughts and vision of his program, many of which I agreed with. I then made some of his thoughts part of our vision. I also recognized that there were things unique to our program that I wanted to incorporate and make our own.

Coach Kunau gave me a book to read at the end of our meeting by Ken Blanchard called *Full Steam Ahead*. This book, which focused on developing and sustaining a compelling vision, was a very useful tool for me to complete our vision.

Building a Culture: Vision, Mission, Core Beliefs

Over the course of the next few weeks, I developed our vision in more depth. I remembered back when I was playing under Coach Plaisance. I recalled all the positive things that happened while playing in his program. The biggest thing I remembered was the relationships between my teammates and I. We had become so close by playing together that it transcended the football field. We would all become good friends, which would continue past our playing days. I would be at some of the other's military and/or college graduations. We would be at each other's weddings. We would be present at the birth of each other's children, attend our kids' birthday parties, invest in each other's businesses, and so on. There were other lessons we all learned about how to be a good citizen, employer/employee, and, overall, a solid, contributing member of society. These were the things that I got out of participating in high school football that I wanted to impress on the young men who played in our program.

From this, I planned a vision that comprised these ideas and the concept of success. I defined what success in our program looked like. This was critical, especially given that in our day and culture, we often define success as winning. This could take the form of a win/loss record or championships in sports. In life, it could mean having a lot of money, a fancy car or a big house, a certain career or job title, or any other material things that people often use to define success. While there is nothing wrong with having all those things, I did not want that to be our definition of success, especially with playing football. If we base our success on wins and losses, what do we tell the players when we lose? Are they not winners because they lost a game? For me, that seemed shallow and very unsustainable. It was much more important to me for the players to give consistently and unselfishly their very best in all they did. This idea came from Coach Wooden, whom I learned about from Coach Brownfield. (See Chapter 1).

Coach Wooden never talked about winning or losing. His sole focus was on each player performing and giving their best effort. If each player could go to sleep at night saying he had, then to him, that was a success. The beautiful part of this definition is that when it's determined and measured this way, success is achievable for everyone. This can happen regardless of skill, talent, or ability.

Another major component of success focuses on the process over the outcome. Too many times, people are so outcome-driven that they forget to focus on the steps that get them to where they want to end up. Success must be a process-orientated endeavor so that one does the work necessary to achieve the desired outcome. So, our definition of success incorporated all these ideas.

For the first 15 years of our program, our vision was to send young men out of our program who would become great husbands, fathers, citizens, and employers/employees. They could do this by consistently and unselfishly giving their best in all they did, thus achieving success, as we defined it. While we emphasized this and taught it year after year, it became apparent to me it was wordy and cumbersome. While all the tenets of our vision were present, it would become challenging for players to remember all of it at once. They could recall bits and pieces of it, especially if prompted by our coaching staff. But I wanted to shorten it and make it more readily accessible to our players. I read Urban Meyer's book, *Above the Line: Lessons in Leadership and Life from a Championship Season*. This allowed me to fine-tune our vision into an easy-to-remember sound bite.

In the book, Coach Meyer explained how the Ohio State football program would go through a culture transformation by hiring Tim and Brian Kight of Focus 3. Their company focuses on leadership, culture, and behavior training. They assisted Coach Meyer in strengthening their already solid culture. They did this by giving them simple concepts of behavioral expectations that would drive their culture.

I became fascinated with the ideas shared by the father (Tim) and son (Brian) team and would reach out to them. I connected with Tim, and through several phone conversations and emails, he helped me understand and define what we wanted as our vision. All we want for our players is for them to be the best version of themselves.

Through this simple statement, "Be the best version of you," we could state what we wanted from our players. This became our vision statement. Now, this doesn't mean we did not explain what that meant. But it meant that our players had a quick, simple, and easy-to-remember statement that defined our vision. Tim would share some more concepts and ideas that would help us refine our culture, which I will share later in the chapter.

MISSION: BUILD A CHAMPION FOR LIFE (YOUR WHY)

> *"To prepare young men who will consistently and unselfishly give their very best in anything they do for the rest of their lives."*

If our vision addresses the "what," then the mission addresses the "why." Your mission should state the purpose of why you are doing what you are doing. They each serve a different purpose. Your vision statement guides your organization as it moves forward and strives to achieve what you have stated. Your mission serves as a daily reminder of why we are doing what we are doing. For us, the mission was very clear. We wanted to build a champion for life. A champion is someone who has achieved a level of excellence. In our world, this equates to some form of athletic success. We wanted to go beyond being a champion on the field and extend this concept to all areas of our player's lives. Our mission is a daily reminder to everyone associated with our program. We are striving to build young men who will pursue becoming a champion in all aspects of life. Athletics, academics, personal choices, home, work, community, and any other areas that they are involved in. We want the players to ask themselves, is what I'm doing getting me closer to becoming a champion?

CORE BELIEFS:

> *Relentless Effort, Competitive Greatness, & Unconquerable Character (Your How)*

Once our vision and mission were in place, it came time to determine our core values. Your core values determine "how" you're going to live out your vision and mission. They are the day-to-day behaviors that need to be shown by everyone associated with your program.

When I sat down to decide what I wanted our core values to be, I focused on the areas that mattered most. I wanted our program to be based on beliefs that encapsulated everything we were trying to accomplish. Again, I leaned on the ideas that Coach Kunau conveyed to me in our meeting. We used this as our blueprint. We chose genuine love for others, unconquerable character, academic greatness, and competitive greatness. I taught each of these values to our players over the years, and we spent a lot of time investing in different ways to get them taught. We strived to live them out. I felt like we were doing a good job of communicating these values, but over time, I noticed that our effectiveness in teaching them became stale.

Building a Culture: Vision, Mission, Core Beliefs

As mentioned earlier, I reached out to Tim Kight and shared our vision, mission, and core values. Through our discourse, he helped me to reshape our core values into core beliefs. He showed me how to streamline and describe behaviors that our players needed to show to live out our vision and mission. Once our conversation ended, a few days later, I met with our coaching staff. We, as a collective group, hashed out what we believed was the best way to get our players to execute our core beliefs.

The first thing we did was list the beliefs that were the most important for our players to show in all phases of their lives. We had a good starting point in that we had our four core values, but we wanted to simplify them to just three. By doing this, we could merge concepts and guarantee that our players covered everything we wanted them to do.

Next, we would identify three distinct areas where we expected behaviors to be shown. We listed the field/weight room, the classroom/on campus, and at home/in the community. I felt that by creating these three distinct *areas*, we were eliminating any chance of a player saying he didn't know that our beliefs applied to all areas of their lives. We then listed the *behaviors* we wanted our players to show in each of these areas as they pertained to the core belief. They needed to be very specific and measurable so that we could see it from the players and we, as coaches, could live it out. We identified the *outcome* we expected to see once they carried the behaviors out. We had created our core beliefs based on Urban Meyer's book, our old core values, and conversations with Tim Kight.

CORE BELIEF #1: RELENTLESS EFFORT

Relentless effort means doing everything in your physical and mental power to give your best effort to any endeavor. However, it doesn't end there. We expect them to give their best while being relentless, single-minded, and never giving up, even in the face of insurmountable odds, with a smile on their face. It's a mindset that requires them to have grit, guts, and a dogged determination that will not stop, no matter how hard it gets. It's like Arnold Schwarzenegger's character in *The Terminator*. He just keeps coming no matter what you throw in front of him. A few years ago, I came across the Finnish word "Sisu" in the book *The Smartest Kids in the World* by Amanda Ripley and, more recently, in the book *Grit: The Power of Passion and Perseverance* by Angela Duckworth. The term describes a cultural belief embedded in Finland's culture. The closest word in English is grit, but that doesn't do it justice. Sisu is the idea of extraordinary effort and determination in the face of adversity, even if knowing the result will be a failure. It defines a mindset that people have regardless of what obstacles, challenges, or failures they experience. It's the idea that no matter what happens, they will endure and accept it with no excuses. This idea expresses a level of toughness, determination, and resolve that few words in the English language can provide. A phrase we often use to express this idea of relentless effort in the face of adversity is "embrace the suck." I borrowed the phrase from the U.S. Navy SEALS, the elite military unit that some say puts its candidates through the toughest screening process on the planet. Going through BUD/S (Basic Underwater Demolition/SEAL) training, the candidates are often wet, cold, and sandy. Candidates push themselves to the mental and physical limits the human body can endure, all while being sleep-deprived. The training sucks. In order to motivate and push the candidates to endure and not quit (i.e., ring the bell), the phrase "embrace the suck" has become their theme. It connotes a mental picture of learning to not only accept the pain and struggle but to enjoy it. When you combine all these elements, you get the type of mindset we wanted our players to display.

Once we defined what this core belief looked like, we then began brainstorming how their behavior would show. We used the three areas of a player's life (field/weight room, classroom/on campus, home/community).

On the field and in the weight room, we want our players to give us maximum effort for four to six seconds from point A to B, plus two more steps. The average play in football lasts four to six seconds. The sound bite for this is "4 to 6, A to B, plus 2," which is a simple way for the players to remember what we want. This is a very specific and measurable behavior that we expect our players to execute while playing their position on the field and while working out. An example of this would be a wide receiver running his route at full speed, catching the ball thrown to him, and trying to get as many yards as possible. In the weight room, it may look like a player doing a hang-clean exercise by exploding their hips, catching the bar in the rack position, and repeating the movement until they complete the lift with relentless effort.

In the classroom and on campus, we want the players to be on time, complete all assignments, and be prepared for tests. This would ensure that they understand what our behavioral expectations were for them as students. For them to succeed in their academics, these needed to be done with relentless effort. We are firm believers that outstanding students make outstanding football players.

At home and in the community, we want the players to give their best in anything that is asked of them. This meant that if their parents asked them to complete a chore or help around the house, they would do so with great effort and do so with a joyful heart. In the community, it means being a good, polite, and respectful person.

The outcome we expect to achieve by making a relentless effort is to be mentally and physically prepared for any situation we face. It's one of the few areas (effort) that is 100% within their control.

Relentless Effort
Behavioral Expectations

1. We will go as hard as we can for four to six seconds from point A to B (field/weight room)
2. We will be on time, complete all assignments, and be prepared for tests. (in class)
3. We will try our best in all aspects of life. (home/community)

Outcome we achieve: We will be mentally and physically prepared for any situation we face.

Sound bite: four to six, A to B, plus 2

CORE BELIEF #2: COMPETITIVE GREATNESS

Our second core belief involves the concept of competition. Competing in sports is one of the core tenets and goes without saying, but we needed to define what that would look like to our players. I read Pete Carroll's book, *Win Forever: Live, Work, and Play Like a Champion*. This concept fueled his resurgence as a coach following his firing from the New England Patriots in 2000. While taking a break, he did a lot of soul-searching and identified competition as the backbone of what he believed in. He felt this was vital to achieving success. He went to USC, winning 3 National Championships in his tenure (2003, 2004, and 2005) and appearing in a fourth National Championship game, a loss to Texas in the 2006 BCS title game. I visited the USC program while he was head coach and saw the intense competition among the players and coaches. Everything they did had some element of competition infused into it. It was exciting and infectious to witness. Players ran around the field during drills, group, and team periods, hooting and hollering. They were excited about everything they did. It sold me that competition was critical to get the players to a level of excellence that we wanted them to display.

Besides competing with others in team settings, it was imperative that we got the players to compete against themselves as well. This is doing everything they can to be better at whatever task is in front of them as compared to their own personal best. Much like a track athlete, a swimmer, or any other activity that requires a time or measurement to be beaten, we wanted the players to top their best mark, even if only by a little. By doing this, they will see improvement and betterment in what they are being asked to do.

To be competitive on the field and the weight room, we had to ensure that the players understood what that meant and how to do it. We determined that for our players to achieve competitive greatness, they needed to understand and execute the fundamentals and responsibilities of their position. The sound bite for this is "know and do your job." Again, this gives the players a very clear picture of what behaviors they need to do to achieve this. We expect each player to know where to line up. They need to know what to do based on the assignment given to them on the play, how to perform the technique and fundamentals, and how to execute all of them. In the weight room, it means they know what the lift is, how to perform it correctly, and how to complete it.

In the classroom, they will show an ability to learn and grow from their success and failures. This means that they will try their best in their academic performance. They do this by studying, completing their assignments, and being unafraid to take chances in doing what's being asked of them. They will understand that learning is a growth process. This requires them to ask questions for clarification. They must attempt to answer questions they may not know the answer to. It also means that they may not do assignments correctly. We want our athletes to understand that growth often happens because of our failures. I have often said to the players that we learn a lot more from our mistakes than from our successes. This can only happen if we have a growth-oriented mindset. Carol Dweck's book *Mindset: The Psychology of Success* explains the difference between growth and a fixed mindset.

After hearing a TED Talk with Dr. Dweck explaining how this concept works, I became fascinated to teach our players the difference between the two mindsets. People who have a fixed mindset believe that talent, skill, ability, and intelligence are qualities you are born with, and an individual can't do anything to improve upon them. You either have *it* or you don't. It creates a very negative mental state of mind and prohibits individuals from even attempting to improve because they believe they can't. They are afraid to ask questions, make mistakes, or fail because they feel embarrassed or inadequate. A growth intention mindset is one in which a person believes an individual can improve in all these areas. They are not afraid to take chances and challenge themselves because they understand that to grow, you must push your limits, which may mean you fail. For them, a growth intention mindset equals improvement because they accept that failure leads to getting better.

At home or in the community, competitive greatness means we will look for opportunities to serve and help others. This is very similar to the relentless effort, with the subtle difference of being active and seeking ways to better the lives of those around us. It means doing things around the house without being asked and volunteering to help with a local charity. Or just helping people who need help in the community. This won't happen unless you are looking to help and serve.

The outcome we aim to achieve is to give our best consistently and unselfishly in all we do for the better of those who are in our lives.

Competitive Greatness Behavioral
Behavioral Expectations:

1. We will understand/execute the fundamentals/responsibilities of our position. (field)
2. We will show an ability to learn/grow from our successes and failures. (class)
3. We will look for opportunities to serve and help others. (home/community)

Outcome we achieve: We will consistently and unselfishly give our very best in all we do.

Sound bite: Know and Do Your Job

CORE BELIEF #3: UNCONQUERABLE CHARACTER

Our third core belief involves our players having unconquerable character. This idea involves the players making good choices both on and off the field. I am a firm believer that everyone is born with a moral compass, in which they know the difference between right and wrong. This, of course, doesn't mean that we always choose the right one, but it means that everyone can discern the difference between the two.

Several years ago, I went to visit with the football staff at Texas A&M University. During this visit, which was to learn about their defense, I visited with their inside linebacker coach, Dat Nguyen. He was a former standout player for the Aggies and the NFL Dallas Cowboys. While speaking to him about drills and techniques, coaching philosophy came up, and we began discussing developing young men. He shared with me his mantra for the guys he coached, which focused on decisions, choices, and consequences. His players used each one of these steps to have a systematic way of making wise choices. Each day, we are all presented with multiple decisions to make, which require us to make choices. The last component of this equation, consequences, is often overlooked or ignored, especially by young people. It was this concept that we wanted our players to understand that every choice they make will have consequences. The challenge is to ensure, to the best of their ability, that each choice they make leads to a positive consequence. The choices they make often reveal the character that they have. So, for us, it was critical that we taught character so that our players have the knowledge and wisdom to make good choices.

On the field or in the weight room, we will use positive and encouraging words with our teammates. This is how we display an unconquerable character. The sound bite for this is to "love people," which starts with player-to-player communication on our own team. We show our love by speaking a language that uplifts our teammates, not putting them down. Often, in a team sports environment, players will joke with, make fun of, or "hack" on each other. They may view joking about each other as good-natured and fun-loving, especially among players who have known each other for quite some time. It can sometimes manifest itself into mean-spirited and hurtful words. It is essential that our players understand you cannot make fun of or joke with players with whom you have not developed a relationship. Those receiving negative words, phrases, expressions, or nicknames disguised as jokes may not welcome them. It can have an adverse effect on the individual and the team. We want our players to be positive with the words they use. No one on our team should feel isolated, picked on, or alienated. We can only accomplish this if we use positive language.

The second part of this concept involves the use of encouraging words. This is especially true when players make a mistake on the field. Much of the time, when a player makes a mistake, they know it already and feel bad enough without having his teammates call him out on it. This does nothing to make the player feel better, confident, or accepted by his teammates and, in fact, may lead to more mistakes being committed. We want our players to lift each other up, especially when mistakes happen, using genuine and encouraging words. This will make the player who committed the mistake feel better. It will also give him the confidence needed to move on and focus on the next task asked of him. We want everyone on the team to feel loved, accepted, and part of the team. This becomes easier when everyone is using a loving, positive, and encouraging tone when speaking to each other.

A third component of communicating with our teammates is helping each other to get better with our words. Giving encouraging feedback while performing tasks can help us enhance our team's communication. Several years ago, when I was an assistant coach, our team was taking part in a passing league contest during the summer. We were getting outscored. With the game out of reach for us, the other team began rotating in younger, less experienced players. When this happens, typically, the starters will go off to the side, relax, and hang out until the contest is over. But this team was different. It amazed me as I watched the starters stay engaged and "coach up" the younger, less experienced players. They were giving constant feedback to the other players after every play, pouring themselves into them and making sure they understood what to do. I found this very inspirational and would use this example for our own players. I want them to be each other's best advocates and helpers. There is something powerful about watching players help players get better and grow. They can only do this if they have an unconquerable character that manifests itself in speaking positive and encouraging words.

In the classroom, demonstrating an unconquerable character means our players are men of integrity. This is done when performing their academic tasks. This means that they are not cheating, which nowadays has become much more difficult to manage. Players do not see copying someone else's homework, essays, projects, or any other assignment given to them as cheating. They view it as getting the work completed and turned in. It has become an issue for teachers. We have to use creativity with our assignments to ensure that the students are doing the work themselves. Our players know the difference between cheating and not cheating, but getting them to do their own work is a constant challenge. Cheating on quizzes and tests is another area we stress our players to abstain from. We stress to them that cheating is a shortcut when you have not prepared for assessments that are given. It also reveals a lack of character and integrity when you choose to cheat. We try to use life examples where cheating has led to failure and relate it to their academic experience. Sometimes, this is effective, while at other times, it is not. We stress to our players the importance of having integrity and not sacrificing it for a grade.

The last area we stress unconquerable character is at home and in the community by getting them to do the right thing at the right time. Many years ago, I heard Steve Bogan, who at the time was the head coach at South Hills High School in West Covina, California, speak at a coaching clinic. He made a statement that made a lasting impression on me as it pertains to player conduct and behavior. He said, "We tell our players to do what they are supposed to do, how they are supposed to be doing it when they are supposed to be doing it." I felt the simplicity of this statement had such power in explaining what we wanted from our players. We expect them to be good people, living a life of integrity and treating people with respect and love. The only way to do this is by talking to them about life choices and role-playing situations they may face to teach them how to respond. In their homes, we talk to them about how they speak to their parents or authority figures and how they should be cognizant of the words and tone they use to speak. We want them to show respect and honor their parents by their actions and words. Honesty is essential in their interactions with parents (or other authority figures) to build and maintain trust. In relation to siblings, we stress to them the need to be role models for younger ones and supportive of older ones.

In the community, we want our players to understand that they represent our program. Anything they say or do in public will either bring pride or embarrassment to the team. We talk to them about having situational awareness when talking in public. This is especially true when they are with their friends at a restaurant, store, park, or anywhere else. We want them to ensure they are not using foul language or coarse speech. We stress to the players that even though they may not be wearing our school gear or uniform, people know who they are and that they are part of our program. For the conversations they have in public while amongst their friends, we ask them to imagine that their grandmother was there with them. Would she be proud of the language, speech, and topics being discussed? If the answer is yes, then carry on, but if the answer is no, then it needs to stop. Part of this involves talking about issues that relate to race, ethnicity, religion, and sexual orientation. We do this to ensure that they understand what is/what is not OK to say in public. We have taught them that speaking negatively about race, sexuality, religion, or politics is not acceptable. The world has become divisive. It has weaponized language to attack individuals or groups who do not represent us or share the same view as us. But that does not grant us permission to partake in it. We want our players to be people that members of the community are proud to know and walk away thinking that we are outstanding young men.

Another area in which we expect our players to show unconquerable character is in the choices they make when not around any adults or authority figures. We talk about criminal behavior and stress the importance of being a good citizen by obeying the law. Stealing, selling drugs, robbing, or any other activity that may cause an arrest and/or conviction is unacceptable in our program. We have been very fortunate over the years in that we have not had too many issues in this area, but we discuss it with our players.

The biggest area of concern and discussion with our players has involved the use of alcohol and drugs. This is a constant battle that we, as adults, are fighting with our young people today. It is everywhere, and the temptations are very real and powerful. We are reminding our players of the dangers involved in this type of activity and to make wise choices by avoiding the use of them at all costs. I will talk about this subject in more depth later in the book. But understand, it is the single biggest challenge in character development that we spend the most time talking about.

Another topic under this core belief relates to who the players choose to spend their free time with. People often think that athletes all hang out with each other when not practicing or working out together. While this may be true sometimes, our players often have other friends who are not part of our program. There is nothing wrong with this.

We want our players to be well-rounded individuals who have all kinds of different friend groups they belong to. We are talking to them about who they hang out with and what they are doing with them. Are those people providing temptations difficult to resist? Are they encouraging them to do things they know are wrong? If the people our players choose to hang out with are not bringing out the best in them, they should avoid being with them. "Show me who your friends are, and I'll tell you who you are." While our players may be innocent of nefarious activities, the people they hang out with may not be. This can be very difficult for young people to accept as they may feel like they are abandoning their "friends." We stress the importance of being with people who are going to make them a better person.

The last topic of unconquerable character in the community relates to how we treat women. Our culture has dehumanized women and made them more of an object for men's pleasure rather than humans who deserve to be treated with our utmost respect. We hear it in speech used by men, the song lyrics played, and the images we see on billboards, magazines, television, and movies. It is critical that our young men see and treat women as they would want their mothers, sisters, and other family members treated. We ask them to be very conscious of the language they use when speaking to or about women. Anything that implies women are less than us as men is unacceptable. Women are to be treated as equals and respected because they are human beings like us.

In dating, we talk to the players about how to treat a young lady. We ask them to do three things. Treat them with respect. Be honest with your intentions. Seek relationships that will benefit both them and the person they are dating in a positive and healthy way. This involves relationships that may become physical as well. We talk about relationships that may become sexual. We discuss the difficulties and challenges that may arise when pursuing this type of activity. While we recognize that "it takes two to tango," we stress to our players that we are in control of our own bodies and what we choose to do with them. We want our young men to make wise choices in this area to ensure they are not putting themselves in a compromising position.

In terms of non-consensual sexual activity, we tell our players that there is never a time when it is OK to force ourselves on another person. No means no, period. We talk about them controlling their emotions and that it is never OK to put your hands on someone against their will, whether done in jest or out of anger. Dating violence is nothing new, but we want our players to be aware of the implications that will arise if they choose to do this. Not just the legal ramifications but because, as a man, we should never put our hands on a woman because it is the wrong thing to do. For us, treating women with respect and honor is something that we take seriously. Any violations of this will be grounds for immediate termination from our program.

Unconquerable Character

Behavioral Expectations:

1. We will communicate positively/use encouraging words with our teammates. (field)
2. We will show integrity when doing our schoolwork. (classroom)
3. We will "do the right thing" at the "right time." (home/community)

Outcome we achieve: We will have a genuine love for one another and have a heart of integrity.

Sound bite: Love People

SUMMARY OF BUILDING A CULTURE

Vision, mission, and core beliefs. When you put all this together, you have our culture. As the head coach, it is my job to implement, maintain, and enforce the standard. Our behaviors show that our culture is being carried out. In the end, you're either getting better or you're getting worse. No one stays the same. It is through our culture that we believe we are getting better every day.

5

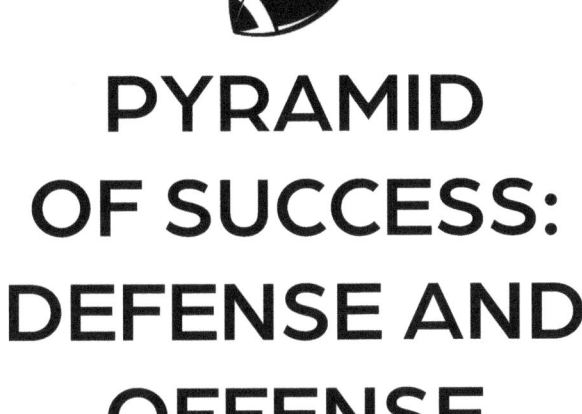

PYRAMID OF SUCCESS: DEFENSE AND OFFENSE

"To know thyself is the beginning of wisdom."

—SOCRATES

As a student of the game, I have invested a lot of time attending coaches' clinics, reading books, listening to podcasts, watching videos, and speaking to coaches to learn as much as I can about the game I love. One of the more intriguing aspects of learning about football is all the different philosophies involving schemes. Coaches love to share why they do what they do and what they feel is critical to have either a successful offense or defense. The schemes of each coach may differ, but their underlying philosophy remains the same. What I discovered the more I studied was that each of these different coaches had a lot of superb ideas. But there was no structure or organization to their philosophies that made sense to me. That's not to say that the coaches I listened to didn't have a structure. I just could not see one that made sense to me in a concise, easy-to-understand, and easy-to-teach manner. Having a philosophy is essential, but if your coaches and players can't articulate it in a simple, easy-to-explain manner, it's just words on paper. For me, I wanted everyone involved to speak it, but most of all, I wanted them to implement it. This was why and how the Pyramids for Defensive and Offensive Success were born (see Appendix for full visual).

DEFENSIVE PYRAMID OF SUCCESS

As discussed in Chapter 2, I learned about Coach Wooden's Pyramid of Success, which he used for his teams while coaching basketball at UCLA. The Pyramid took all the essential ideas of running a successful team and placed them in a visual (the Pyramid) that was easy to understand. Each block of the Pyramid has a word that describes a key idea that is essential for the team to live out and do to be the best version of themselves. It was this visual that I used to implement what I believed were all the essential concepts in our defensive philosophy.

The Objective

The key statistic for determining a defensive unit's effectiveness was scoring defense. If the offense does not score, you have a greater probability of winning the game. With this in mind, it was paramount to place this at the top of our pyramid. We made it our priority to keep teams out of the end zone and not stress about other statistics (rushing yards, passing yards, total offense, 3rd down conversions, etc.). While these stats are important to different parts of the Pyramid, we felt that keeping them out of the end zone needed to be the top priority. For this reason, *No TDs* are at the top of our pyramid and are called the Objective.

The Apex

The next two blocks, which we call the Apex, are *Stop the Run* and *Limit Explosive Plays*. These are the simplest ways for an offensive unit to move the ball down the field and get into a position to score.

The first block, *Stop the Run,* focuses on us, effectively preventing the other team from running the ball. Running the ball by either handing or pitching it to another player or the quarterback running it himself is the easiest way to attack open space. Running the ball allows an offense to move the ball down the field with little to no risk of turning the ball over. If the offensive line and perimeter players block well, running can demoralize the defense. There is a feeling of helplessness by defensive coaches and players when a defensive unit can't stop the run of an offense. Therefore, coaches and players on defense must do whatever it takes to stop the rushing attack of an offensive unit.

Stopping the run accomplishes several things: it makes the offense one-dimensional; it takes away their ability to control the clock; it limits their ability to dictate the pace of the game. And it frustrates the offensive unit's ability to have confidence that they can simply run the ball. We do this in several ways.

First, we identify what the team's favorite rushing plays are and how they will most likely block them against us. Second, using our base scheme and calls, we determine how we are going to "fit-up" our players to the scheme of the play to ensure we are sound in our defense of it. Third, we will come up with solutions to defend the play should our base scheme prove ineffective in defending it. This could involve changing players, alignments, or running a blitz that may disrupt what they are trying to do. Finally, we stress to our players the importance of taking their favorite run plays away by executing the call(s) we have made to defend it. They must understand that what we have called takes that play away, but only if the players execute the fundamentals and techniques to do so.

We must eliminate the offense's ability to run the ball and make them one-dimensional (i.e., force them to pass the ball). There are very specific things we can do to address this. We create film cut-ups and review their favorite run plays in class, so our players understand the scheme. Next, we walk through the schemes on the field, especially with our offensive scout team players, so they make it look exactly like the opponent. We then conduct inside and outside run periods (9 on 7) to represent the defense versus the plays and mix in the opponent's favorite run plays in the entire team scrimmages. To effectively limit what the offense can do, we must put a premium on stopping the run.

The second block of the Apex is to *Limit Explosive Plays*. We define an explosive run play as 12 yards or more and an explosive pass play as 16 yards or more. I don't recall where I heard or read it, but the theory is that if an offensive unit has two explosive plays on a drive, they will score (either a field goal or touchdown) 80% of the time. If they have more than that, the percentage goes up even higher. So, limiting explosive plays ensures that the offense must consistently move the ball in small chunks. This can be very difficult to do over the course of the game. The question becomes, how do we limit explosive plays? There are several factors involved in doing this.

You need to identify their explosive players, identify their explosive plays, and then design schemes to limit the productivity of both. First, make sure that the defense lines up correctly to defend the formation.

The easiest way for an explosive play to happen is being misaligned, and the offense exploits it simply because we were not where we were supposed to be. The second way is to ensure that we get the ball carrier down on the ground as soon as possible. This requires us to be sure tacklers and prevent YAC (yards after contact) yardage from happening. The third and final way to prevent explosive plays is to take the ball away from the offense. If they don't have the ball, they can't carry out explosive plays. There are very specific things we do to work on defending explosive plays. We create film cut-ups and review their explosive plays in the classroom. Next, we walk through the schemes of their explosive plays on the field. Then, we conduct special category segments (we call these special cat periods) in practice to address these plays. Last, we work on techniques that help reduce explosive players' skill sets (for example, if a player uses a stiff arm, work on drills to defend it). By carrying out these various aspects, we attempt to limit explosive plays, which we feel limit their ability to score.

The Core

The next row of the Pyramid, called the Core, comprises three blocks: *Block Destruction, Perfect Tackling,* and *Create Takeaways*. We place them at the center of the Pyramid because they make up the core of our foundation. Without these, we could not stop the run and limit explosive plays.

The first block focuses on *block destruction*. This means getting off of an offensive player who is attempting to block us, thus preventing us from being able to make a tackle. We stress attacking half the man, (who is trying to block us) by using leverage and hips for explosive movement, striking violently and locking our arms out to create separation. Once separation has occurred, we have them use their eyes to find the ball carrier. Next, we disengage using either a throw-by (some call this trash the blocker), a rip move, or an overhand punch (like a swim move but much tighter). Each technique is applicable based on where the ball is, how best to get there, and finally, what their comfort level is using the techniques. Let the player use whichever one works best for them. Whichever technique they use, it must be done with extreme violence. There are very specific things we do to work on block destruction. We introduce and teach the techniques in mass to the players during winter and spring. Next, we create drill circuits that work on blocking destruction. We do position-specific drill work. We do group periods that work on blocking destruction, incorporating multiple players. Last, we must get the blocker off of us so we can execute a tackle on the ball carrier.

The second block is a *perfect tackle*. Teaching tackling has changed over the years. Long gone are the days when we teach players to "stick their nose in there" or "get your head across the bow." This involves the use of the head, which is dangerous and can lead to head injuries. Concussions are serious business. Keeping the head out of the tackle has been a priority in our program for years because of the information we have on TBI (traumatic brain injury) and CTE (chronic traumatic encephalopathy). We have always been cognizant of teaching our players, regardless of where I coached, to keep their heads up and see what they hit.

Our transformation into the shoulder-led rugby-style tackle started with the Seattle Seahawks. Head Coach Pete Carroll made a video on what he called "Hawk Tackling." This concept spread like wildfire across all levels of coaching. We implemented it. But it wasn't until we became a client of the Atavus Tackling System that our method of teaching and use of drills took on a whole new level of tackling.

Coach Rex Norris was the lead instructor over football for teaching tackling at Atavus, a Seattle based Rugby Training company. He was instrumental in our transition into teaching rugby-style tackling. His online training platform was second to none. It allowed us to learn, teach, and implement the technique. All the drills involve low intensity and low contact. You can do them quickly and easily without helmets or shoulder pads. Designing drills this way allows the players to really focus on the technique rather than the collision, which makes them much better tacklers.

The key tenets of a perfect tackle in the open field begin with taking the proper angle and maintaining leverage. We do this while tracking the near hip of the ball carrier and coming to balance once we are near impact. It then involves the player stepping with the near foot, timing the strike on the ball carrier with the near shoulder on the near hip. Next, we place the head behind the ball carrier (my cheek on his butt cheek), keeping the head out of contact. Once the shoulder meets the hip, we finish the tackle by wrapping the ball carrier's thighs and squeezing them together. We finish by running our feet until the ball carrier is on the ground. This will mean our momentum will carry us into a "gator roll," also known as a wrap-and-roll tackle.

There are examples when we are in close quarters that our players will not have time to get their shoulder to the hip. But we still teach keeping the head behind and out of contact. We finish by wrapping the ball carrier and driving him with our feet until he falls or the whistle blows. Whichever situation happens, both stop the offensive player's progress and end the advance of the ball.

There are several ways we teach tackling. Introduce the techniques in mass during the winter and spring. Create several tackling circuits to work the various aspects of tackling and position-specific drills.

By using this system, we have been able to reduce the amount of full contact we have had to use in practice, thus cutting down on injuries. We want our players to be great tacklers, but we also want them healthy enough to play in games. This technique has revolutionized how we teach tackling.

The last block of the core is to *create takeaways*. In football, the ball is everything. If we can protect it on offense, we have a much better chance of advancing it and scoring. On defense, the opposite is true. If we can take it away from our opponent, we have a much better chance of preventing them from scoring. The easiest way to take the ball away is to intercept it. If the ball is in the air, we teach our players that they have just as much a right to the ball as we do, so get it. Once the ball is in the air, we stress our players to try to catch the ball at its height. We don't want the ball coming down, which may give the offensive player a chance to make the catch. Sometimes, intercepting the ball may be difficult. So, we teach our players how to position themselves to intercept it while maintaining the ability to make a tackle if they don't.

The next set of techniques focuses on taking the ball away from the ball carrier once they have possession of it. Creating turnovers involves the second man who reaches the ball carrier executing a "peanut punch," a strip and rip, or a club on the ball. While sometimes a single tackler may cause a turnover, we only stress this if a score is imminent. Examples include the ball carrier about to cross the end zone or catch a ball in the end zone. Another would be a ball carrier that does not see us coming (i.e., sacking a quarterback from behind), or the game situation dictates we need the ball back (i.e., we are behind on the scoreboard, and time is limited in the game).

The first technique is what we call the "peanut punch," made famous by former Chicago Bears defensive back Charles "Peanut" Tillman. He would approach a ball carrier, usually from the front, like in an open-field tackle. He would time up his strike and punch the ball out of the ball carrier's hand while still maintaining a proper position to make a tackle. One area of emphasis we have stressed to the players is for them to use their dominant hand when attempting to punch the ball out. This also works when approaching a player from behind who may not see the defender coming.

Another technique we teach is the strip and rip. This involves the defender using his arm and hand in a downward motion. By getting his hand between the ball and the ribs of the ball carrier, he will violently rip the ball out. We often use this when we are approaching a ball carrier from behind, and we can see the ball. Sometimes, the player's initial downward blow on the ball is enough to get the ball out. But we still stress the rip portion of the technique to ensure maximum effectiveness. Another technique we teach is the club. This usually happens from behind when we cannot see the ball. Because the ball is in the arm of the ball carrier farthest away from us, we teach them to use an uppercut motion to club the ball out. Regardless of the technique used, we ensure the defender is still in a solid position to make the tackle if the ball does not come out.

Finally, once the ball is out of the ball carrier's hand, we will do one of two things. If the ball is on the ground with a lot of other players around, we teach our players to secure the ball and tuck it into the fetal position. We call this a "city" recovery because there is a large crowd around the ball. If the ball is on the ground in the open field (we call this "country" because there is a lot of wide-open space), we teach our players to scoop and score with the ball. When teaching this, we allow the players one shot to scoop up the ball. Any more than that may cause an offensive player to recover the ball. In getting to the side of the ball, bending the knees to crouch down, and scooping the ball up, we lessen the chance of the defender kicking the ball. Once we scoop the ball up, we teach them to score a touchdown.

We teach and drill these techniques by introducing them to the players individually in mass. We also do takeaway circuits emphasizing the various techniques. Last, we stress takeaway attempts in all group and team periods. Making takeaways a significant part of what you do on defense is expensive in terms of practice time, but the investment is worth it come game time.

The Foundation

Several aspects must happen beforehand to put us in a position to destroy blocks, make a tackle, and attempt a takeaway. The bottom row of the Pyramid is called the foundation and comprises four blocks. *Alignment and Assignment, Read Keys (eyes), React (hands and feet technique),* and *Relentless Pursuit.*

The first block revolves around *alignment and assignment.* This means getting in the proper stance and getting lined up correctly. Know the assignment for the call given. Know where to go and what to do once the offense snap the ball. Each position has a unique stance that needs to be executed to allow the player to move with little wasted movement (no false steps) once the ball moves. This goes hand in hand with making sure the player is lined up correctly based on the call, both vertically and horizontally. It is essential to the scheme of the defense that each player knows where to line up. They also need to know what adjustments need to be employed should the offense adjust their alignment. As mentioned earlier, we must line up correctly so that we do not give the offense any "gimmes" because we did not line up incorrectly.

Next, the players need to know, based on the call, what their job is for that given play before the ball moves. This is important because we don't want our players guessing, and we want them to have confidence that they know what to do. By knowing what to do, in theory, they will play faster. Finally, once the ball moves, we expect the players to execute their assignment, go or do what they are supposed to do, and ultimately, get to the ball carrier.

We worked on this block of concepts by going over all this in the classroom using the dry-erase board and film review. Next, we use group walk-through periods on the field and reinforce it by position groups.

The second block is *reading keys*. Having our eyes in the right spot both before and during the play is critical to our success. For any player, the defender must have his eyes locked onto his key so we know when to move, which direction to step, and where to go based on the call given. This concept also involves recognizing the blocking schemes the offense is using. It also involves identifying pass drops of the quarterback and reading route combinations receivers are running. So many times, players will get out of position because they do not focus their eyes on what is happening in front of them. They get caught looking where they shouldn't, which puts them out of position to do their job and make the correct play—having your eyes in the right spot speeds up the decision-making process for the players to accomplish this. We spend a tremendous amount of time teaching our players to get their eyes right to allow them to be successful. We train their eyes in the same way we teach alignment and assignment in the classroom, chalk talk, and film review, then walk-through on the field and position-specific drill work.

The third block, which is closely connected to using their eyes, is to *react with the hands and feet technique*. We have an expression that says, "Using proper eyes, hands, and feet will never get you beat." This requires that the players know what technique and movement pattern to use based on our key read to put us in the best position possible to do the job required. This involves what direction to step in, what block destruction technique to use, and what path needs to be followed to tackle the ball carrier. The position coach covers the bulk of this to ensure the players know exactly what to do for their position.

The last block of the foundation is the *relentless pursuit* of the ball. This is one area that requires zero talent. It relies solely on the effort of the players on the field. Relentless pursuit stresses the players to get to the ball carrier as fast as possible. We stress that all eleven players on the defense must pursue the ball carrier. This needs to be done while taking the proper angle and never following another defender while doing so. They defend all cutback angles and ensure that all players are getting to the ball. This concept of relentless pursuit also allows a player who may have made a mistake in any of the previous blocks discussed to make up for it. By stressing getting to the ball as fast as possible, we can ensure that if one player misses a tackle, there will be multiple defenders in place to secure the tackle.

We stress that if you want to play defense, you must give an all-out effort to get to the ball. We use the term "loaf" to define what it means when a player is not pursuing the ball to our standard. There are plenty of definitions. Not sprinting to the ball and slowing down when running to the ball. Staying on the ground and not getting back up to pursue and getting passed by another player. These are all very easy to see in practice or game films when players are committing a loaf.

We teach pursuit by doing both group and team pursuit drills, but the biggest way we enforce it is in our group periods (inside/outside run and 7-on-7) and full team periods. We dedicate a coach to screaming at the players to get to the ball. I replace any player found guilty of loafing and remind them that if they want to play on defense, they must relentlessly pursue the ball.

This encompasses all that is important to us when playing on defense. Each block stands alone in its importance but makes up the overall philosophy of the defense, which collectively makes us a better unit. To teach and reinforce the entire Pyramid, we start by implementing it in its entirety in the classroom. We will have the players take notes on it and continually review it at the start of each of our team meetings. We will have the players get up and teach it to the unit, we will play games with it, and we will include it in the weekly scouting reports we give the players.

In conclusion, the Defensive Pyramid of success has come with years of experience and knowledge we acquired through the insights of clinics, coaches, and players. This has led us to the conclusion of what experience and knowledge we acquired. The visual gives us a simple way to communicate and teach our players what we need to do. This gives us the best chance possible to defend the variety of offenses we see each season.

OFFENSIVE PYRAMID OF SUCCESS

For the same reason given for why we created the Defensive Pyramid of Success, we did the same for our offensive unit. We wanted to understand what our philosophy and goal for the offensive unit were and put them in the same format so we could articulate them to our players and staff. Many of the goals for offense are in stark contrast to what we want to accomplish on defense.

The Objective

Score is at the top of the Pyramid and is, thus, the main objective of the offensive unit. While we prefer TDs, field goals are acceptable. Whether it is by rushing, passing, or, in a perfect scenario, a combination of the two, we want to score as many points as possible. We try not to get wrapped up in statistics in terms of total yards, 3rd down conversions, pass completions, or any others when conducting our offensive attack.

The end game is simply to score points.

The Apex

The next two blocks are *Four Yards on Run Plays* and *Catch Every Ball on Pass Plays*. These two blocks will give us the highest probability of scoring on any drive and explain why they are the Apex.

Running the ball is the easiest way to move the ball down the field. Handing it off to another player or the quarterback running it himself, we attempt to attack the open bubbles of space that the defense gives us. We can also create space by utilizing our scheme. Whichever we do, moving the ball in this manner accomplishes several objectives. One, it's very simple and effective to move the ball. By handing the ball off and allowing our players to run the ball, we minimize the possibility of a turnover. This assumes the center-to-quarterback and quarterback-to-ball carrier exchange is clean. Second, it allows us to use schemes to best attack the defense. Third, it establishes a dominant posture for the offense when it can effectively move the ball by its rushing attack. Fourth, it opens our passing attack by getting the defenders creeping up or hesitating on pass drops for fear of not being able to stop the run. Finally, it demoralizes a defense when they cannot stop your rushing attack. You want to impose your will on the defensive unit, and running the ball has been our most effective strategy in accomplishing this.

The second block is to *catch every ball on a forward pass plays*. While this sounds simple, there are many factors involved in a pass play to make this happen on a consistent level. The most important aspect of conducting a successful pass play must start with your pass protection. You ensure your quarterback has time to set up and throw, regardless of the type of pass. This begins with identifying the front and potential pass-rush threats. We neutralize them with our offensive lineman and running back if necessary. Whether your pass protection is a partial slide, full slide, or any other, they must account for all potential threats.

If the quarterback does not have time to set up and throw, the play is over before it starts.

Next, you must ensure your quarterback delivers the ball on target. For us, having accurate passing is more important than being able to throw the ball deep down the field. While having the ability to throw deep opens up more opportunities for explosive plays, we don't rely on that. We would rather complete short to intermediate passes and let the receivers do their thing.

Next, your receivers need to ensure that they are laser-focused on catching the ball once we throw at them. Their routes need to be clean, and their body position must be such that they catch the ball or it is incomplete. What's critical for the receivers is that they look the ball into their hands, properly secure it, and then move up the field to gain yards after the catch. Too often, you see receivers try to run and get more yards before they have secured the ball. We stress to them that they must "cook it before they can eat it."

Finally, when attempting to make a catch, they must attempt to catch the ball at its highest point when it comes in their direction. While sometimes the ball is on target, either at their face or their body, sometimes the ball is out in front of them, behind them, or low. Wherever the ball position is when thrown to them, they must try to catch the ball. We stress to the receivers that there is no such thing as a perfect pass, and therefore, they must sell out and make the catch. We tell the receivers that if the ball touches your hands, they must make the catch.

The Core

The next row of the Pyramid, called the core, comprises three blocks, which are *Finish Blocks, Execute Explosive Plays,* and *Protect the Ball*. Each one is critical for us to run the ball and catch every pass.

The first block is called the *finish blocks*. This requires all offensive players not carrying the ball to attack the defenders we assign them to with intensity and vigor. We will use the proper technique and keep a wide base. Next, we will grab hold of the defender's breastplate and drive him. We will finish by shoving them at the whistle. We teach players who are not directly involved in blocking at the point of attack to either carry out a fake or run off a defender. If a player does not have someone to block, we teach them to "look for work" and find someone who is wearing an opposite-color jersey and block them. This ensures that all offensive players are constantly looking for defenders to block. It will also impede the defensive player's ability to make a tackle.

On pass plays, once the ball comes out, we teach all other players to sprint down the field and look for someone to block. You never know if your block is going to spring the ball carrier free for a score.

Finally, we instruct our players to execute their blocks with an attitude of dominance. We want them to physically impose their will on the defenders and to do so relentlessly. We want the defenders to feel a sense of frustration with our effort to keep them away from the ball. This will only happen if our players have an attitude of dominance.

The next block is to *execute explosive plays*. We define an explosive offensive play as a 12-yard rushing play or a 16-yard pass play. If we can put together two explosive plays on a drive, we increase our chances of scoring 80% of the time. Being able to execute explosive plays requires us to not only execute the play correctly but also require an additional component by the ball carrier. We stress we must make the first tackler miss by either making a cut or using a stiff arm, as well as gaining yards after contact (**YAC**). We want our ball carriers to use everything in their power to move or fall forward when getting tackled. When a scrum ensues on any play, we expect any additional players on offense to "move the pile" so we can gain more yards.

The last block is to *protect the ball*. Ball security is our first priority when we have it. We do this by ensuring four points of contact when carrying the ball and having situational awareness of when defenders are coming in to make tackles. We teach our players that when they have the ball, they must secure it with their hand, followed by the wrist locking it into the forearm. With our arm bent at the elbow, we secure it to our rib cage (i.e., four points: hand, wrist, elbow, and ribs).

Finally, it is crucial that our ball carriers have situational awareness. They must know and feel when they are about to get tackled and attempt to protect the ball at all costs. Sometimes, that means using both arms and hands to protect the ball. We do this to ensure that they are not swinging the ball away from their body where it is open for a takeaway attempt. We must maintain possession of the ball, and stressing ball security is how we do this.

The Foundation

The bottom row of our pyramid comprises four blocks: *Knowledge, Aggression, Fundamentals by Position, and Relentless Effort*. While there are plenty of carryovers from one block to the next throughout the Pyramid, we have created this as our foundation.

The first block is *knowledge*. The players need to know the formation so that they can line up correctly. This also includes split adjustments required for not only the formation but also the play called. Some plays require slight adjustments to the offensive line or where the receivers and running back align. These subtle alignments can make all the difference in the success of a play.

They also need to know their assignment on the play as well as how to best execute the fundamentals and techniques it requires. One aspect of this is teaching the players the objective of each play we call so that they know what we are trying to accomplish. By doing this, it presents a clear macro picture of how each player fits into the scheme. Their micro-level of participation ultimately leads to either success or failure.

Finally, they must be able to identify the defensive fronts and coverages. This will allow for adjustments that may need to be made for a play to have success. We spend a lot of time going over all of this in the classroom and during walk-through periods on the field.

The second block is *aggression*. It is important to make this its own block to better stress to the players that we need to play with a posture of dominance. We feel offensive players may play with a passive attitude in attempting to execute plays for fear of doing something wrong if they go "full throttle." We stress to the players that, for us to be successful, we need to do so with an attitude of aggression against the defenders and impose our will on them.

The third block is *fundamentals by position*. The success of each player is determined by the execution of each player's fundamentals unique to their position. Stance, eyes, explosive first steps, footwork, hand placement, and finish are just some basics required for success. Each player must learn what is required for their position and work hard to master the skills needed for them to succeed. It is paramount that if they do not understand what is being asked of them, they seek clarification from their position coach. We rely on our position coaches to teach, drill, and review all steps to make the players successful in their respective positions.

The last block in the foundation is *relentless effort*. We demand that all our players on the offensive unit give every ounce of effort on every single play. This includes an offensive lineman driving their man through the whistle. A running back carrying out his fake. A wide receiver sprinting his route, knowing the play is not coming his way. We understand that even if the player is giving their best effort, they may come up short of achieving the aim of the play, but at least they are giving themselves the best opportunity to succeed. Giving an honest effort will only improve their chances of helping the offense successfully execute the play.

Just like the Defensive Pyramid of Success, we review the Offensive Pyramid with our players in the classroom. We spend time each meeting discussing, reviewing, and teaching the Pyramid to the offensive players. We want the players to understand each block, know the coaching points of each, and be able to explain it to both the coaches and other players. It is critical that each player knows what they need to do within the Pyramid to contribute to the unit's success.

SUMMARY OF PYRAMIDS OF SUCCESS

Whether it's offense or defense, having a philosophy in place that is clear, concise, and easy to remember is critical for both coaches and players. It lays a foundation for what we want to accomplish on each side of the ball. Taking the time to invest in teaching your players what is important about each side of the ball ensures everyone is in alignment. We want there to be no misunderstanding of what is critical for each unit to be successful, but we want our players to know how to do this. The Pyramids give the players the knowledge and confidence needed to make this happen.

6

ASSISTANT COACHES: ONLY THE FEW

"As iron sharpens iron, so one person sharpens another."

—Proverbs 27:17

The toughest part of my job is finding and hiring quality assistant coaches. Year in and year out, it is always a challenge to find people who will come on board and join your program. Ask any head coach of any sport, regardless of level, and they will tell you that their job would not be possible without their assistant coaches. Assistant coaches are the frontline soldiers who carry out the mission of a program. They are the ones doing the day-to-day work. Teaching, mentoring, instructing, correcting, improving, and helping the players grow and achieve success. Their contribution makes the difference between average and great programs.

OUR PROCESS

Once the current season is over, I provide all members of the staff with a post-season questionnaire. I use this for our end-of-the-season evaluation, which usually takes place in December. My goal for us is to grow as a program, and this can only be done when the coaches provide constructive, clear, and honest feedback. I ask them not to pull any punches. I want to know how they felt the season went, what was good, what areas need improvement, and ultimately, anything they feel will make us a better program.

Sometimes, these meetings can be very difficult. It's difficult to hear things that don't paint you in a very positive light. But it's necessary for growth. You may not like what is being said, and you may not agree with it completely, but it's important to give the assistant coaches a forum and a voice. Whatever is said, it is critical that some form of resolution come out of the meeting so that we are all in alignment.

It has not happened too often that we have had the same set of coaches for all three levels from year to year. This is usually because of natural attrition, as well as coaches moving from one level to the next. While some coaches have remained on staff for multiple years, life happens. The need to replace assistant coaches who have moved on becomes necessary. One question I ask is whether they would like to return for the next season. Assuming this is someone I want back on staff if the answer is yes, we move forward and begin laying some groundwork for the off-season. If the answer is no, or if it is someone that I was planning on not keeping, I leave things on good terms. This is always the best way for any relationship to end. Things happen for a variety of reasons. Regardless of the reasons, thank them for their service, wish them the best, and offer to provide any help they may want or need in the future.

For the coaches who expressed a desire to return to the staff, we will use the months of January and February for professional development. We do this by attending clinics while I look for new coaches. As stated, this is one of the most challenging aspects of being a head coach. But if you have a process and you know what you're looking for, it can be very rewarding and surprising who you end up hiring.

WHAT I LOOK FOR WHEN HIRING AN ASSISTANT COACH

Throughout my career, I have had amazing assistant coaches. They understood the importance of their role in the success of what we were trying to accomplish. There have been a variety of personalities and temperaments, but they all shared a common trait: they loved our players and wanted them to be successful. Some coaches I have hired were on-campus teachers, but the bulk of them have been walk-on coaches. In a perfect world, I would prefer to get teachers who coach. This allows for more flexibility to share responsibilities and have an on-campus presence for our players. But finding teachers who coach is a dying breed. It has become increasingly more difficult to do both, especially here in California. With all the requirements our state has made to become a teacher, it can be challenging. Coupled with the increasing number of requirements and training that is placed on becoming a coach, you must really want to be a teacher-coach.

I have been much more successful in hiring walk-on coaches, most of whom have careers. Independent business owners who set their own hours are solid. Law enforcement officers and firefighters are also great hires. Last, any other profession that allows them the flexibility to coach is a great option. Many of the assistants I have had over the years were also former players of mine. This can be especially beneficial as they have a working knowledge of the culture of our community, school, and program.

When it comes to hiring assistant coaches, there are several qualities that I look for. Regardless of whether they are an on-campus or walk-on coach, all of these are equally important.

The first thing I will ask a prospective candidate is, "Why do you want to coach?" The answers to this question can be very revealing in terms of their motives. I want guys who are more interested in developing young men than winning games. While winning games is part of our overall philosophy, it is not the primary purpose of why we do what we do. I want coaches who love coaching a player to be the best version of themselves. They need to have a strong sense of satisfaction watching a player develop because of their instruction. I want coaches who will build relationships with the players that go beyond the field. It is paramount that as an assistant in our program, the coach pours himself into the player that goes beyond just being an on-the-field coach. We are in the business of developing young men, and any assistant we hire needs to know this. This requires them to put their wants and needs secondary to what's best for the players.

The second thing I look for when hiring an assistant coach is availability. Will they put in the time needed to coach our program? Being a coach takes a lot of time, and it's important to me that the people I hire can commit to the time needed to be on our staff. I ask about their family situation (married, single, kids, etc.) and other time commitments that may affect their time availability. I want to ensure that if I hire them, they will put in the work needed for us to be a successful program.

The third quality I look for is humility. I want coaches who have confidence in their abilities but do so with a heart of humility. It is more important that a coach put their own beliefs and opinions second to conform to what we do. This does not mean I do not value or want to hear what they think. But it means that when I make a decision, I need to know that they will be OK with it and move forward with whatever decision I have made. They must put their ego in check. This can be very difficult for a lot of coaches because many of them are alpha males who have powerful feelings about what they believe. While this is not a bad thing, it can become a challenge if a coach is not willing to listen and do what is in the best interest of the program and players.

    The fourth quality I look for in a coach is a willingness to learn and grow. I am not concerned with their experience and knowledge because we can teach the coach what we want to be done and how best to do it. If we hire a coach with little to no experience, it is on us to teach him what we want him to do. It will also require the coach to educate themselves. They do this by attending clinics and watching videos. It will mean meeting with other coaches and reading articles or books to better prepare them to coach for their assignments. Hiring coaches who have coaching experience can be a plus, but it means they have to conform to what needs to be done. This does not mean we want robots, but it means we want coaches who can take their previous experience and integrate it into what we need from them. If the coach has extensive experience in another system, this can be a hindrance to what we need from them. It may cloud their ability to see the merit of why we do things the way we do them. The best scenario would be for an experienced coach to take his previous knowledge and merge it with what we need, which will make us a better program.

    Finally, one pitfall is the coach who feels he has nothing new to learn. Often, especially with coaches who have been doing it for a long time, there is an air of arrogance that can develop and prevent them from being willing to learn. This can be a major hindrance to growth and lead to coaches becoming stagnant in what they do, as well as a challenge to work with. For us, we want growth-minded coaches who are always looking for ways to improve what they do. This can come from learning something new or by receiving validation that what they are doing is on point. Whichever happens, we want our assistants to constantly improve, and this can only be done when the coach has a heart that is willing.

Along with these qualities, I will also ask the candidates a series of questions. Most of which have nothing to do with their knowledge of the scheme or coaching a specific position. Each of these questions reveals self-awareness in the coach and gives me a much clearer picture of who the person is. I love to ask coaches what they feel their strengths are and areas they feel they need to improve upon. This gives me some insight into their state of mind regarding their abilities. It also provides awareness of shortcomings that they feel need to be addressed. If a coach can't give me any areas of improvement, this causes me to pause in the hiring process because it reveals that they don't think they have any need for growth.

I like to ask them how a former player might describe them as a coach. This is a very thought-provoking question. It requires the coach to be very aware of their previous experiences and to be honest with themselves. Another question I like to ask is what their favorite and least favorite part of coaching is. This may reveal their intentions and why they coach, as well as give some insight into what they may struggle with within your program. I will ask them what unique characteristics they can contribute to our program. This is always a fun question because coaches come in all shapes and sizes and have many life experiences that can improve our program.

The final set of questions I will ask has to do with coaching on the field. I will ask what positions they would like to coach and the level they would like to work on. If we have a specific need for a coach, we will try to fill that position with someone who has experience in coaching it, but it's not a deal breaker if they don't. For me, it's more important that I have quality coaches who work well with others. They need to have the will to learn and have a desire to see players improve, regardless of position and level. While I try to meet their requests and desires, I also need to balance that with the needs of the program. I will also ask what their future goals are in coaching. Do they have a desire to be a coordinator? Do they want to be a head coach? Or are they content with being a position coach? This is always good to know moving forward so you can help them achieve their short and long-term goals.

When you put all this together, you are getting a coach who is going to be a team player who gets along with the other coaches on the staff. They will do the best job they can with the assignment they have and will represent our program in the best light possible. While there are no guarantees, look for these qualities, ask the right questions, and trust that the answers are honest. You will inevitably get someone on your staff who will make you better as a coach and contribute to the overall growth of the players in your program.

WHAT ARE MY EXPECTATIONS OF OUR ASSISTANT COACHES ONCE ON STAFF?

With all our coaches' assignments, levels, and positions set, I am ready to conduct our first coaches' meeting in March. This will be for the upcoming season's campaign. It was during this meeting that I laid out my expectations for the staff.

Chain of command

The first order of business is to communicate our chain of command to the entire staff. The chain of command lets everyone know who is in charge of meetings, weight room, practice, or any other activity if I cannot be present. Our chain of command starts with the head coach, then the assistant head coach, and finally, the associate head coach.

There are not too many team-related activities for which the head coach should not be present. But, if you are going to be late, have to leave early, or not be present at all, have your leadership structure already established. This way, everyone knows, and things can continue smoothly.

Points of contact

The second area of structure I communicate is the points of contact for offense, defense, and special teams. The importance of this is for coaches on all three levels to know who to go to should they have questions regarding a particular aspect of one of the three units. By identifying who oversees each unit, our staff has confidence that each point of contact will clarify anything related to that unit and can cover position-specific fundamentals of the scheme. Although we have identified who oversees each unit, our staff can also consult other coaches who coach in each of the units. We have identified the supervisor of each unit, and our staff can also consult with other coaches who work in those units. But it means that the point of contact has the last word on any issues, or questions that may arise. We have found this to be very helpful in maintaining continuity between all three levels.

Staff-to-staff expectations

Once we communicate this, we will begin going over expectations for the staff. I want each of them to respect one another and enjoy being around each other. We give up a lot of time, energy, money, etc., so it is prudent that we all get along and enjoy each other's company. In the end, all I want is for our coaches to get along with one another and have fun being around each other. I will begin by asking each of them to state why they are coaching. We should all be here for the same reasons: love of the game, working with young men, camaraderie with fellow coaches, and the challenge of coaching. This is a unifying activity to get all of us on track for the season. Next, I will go over our vision, mission, and core beliefs (see Chapter 4). For the returning staff members, it serves as a reminder of what our program is all about, while for the new members, it is an indoctrination of why we do what we do.

WHAT COACHES AND PLAYERS SHOULD EXPECT FROM EACH OTHER

I will then go over what we, the coaches, should expect from the players. We expect them to show up each day with a great attitude and provide themselves (and us) with a great effort. We want them to be prepared and show that they care about their teammates in the program and respect the work that we, as coaches, are putting in to help them. The players expect us as coaches to show we care about them as people first players second. They want to know that we are not using them for our own advancement or fulfillment. This experience is about them and their teammates, not our win-loss record.

Loyalty

I will then go over what I expect from them as assistant coaches. The most important expectation I have is loyalty. Coaches come from different backgrounds and have different views. However, as the head coach, it is my responsibility to lead the program. I want their thoughts, opinions, and suggestions. The insight they may want to provide that they feel will improve the various aspects of our program is welcome. I don't want a bunch of "yes" men; however, I will need to make a final decision, and once I do, I need them to be supportive of that and move on. If they disagree with a decision I have made, that's fine. I have no ego (at least, I think I don't), and I can live with their hurt feelings. If their disagreement leads to negative behavior or goes against what I ask, their participation on our staff may end. I stress to them that I want everyone to be a part of the program and make it theirs, but this needs to happen under the umbrella of my direction and the decisions I make.

Show Up

Next, I stress the importance of being at all team functions, which include meetings, practice, or any other team-related activities. This works with what they have stated their availability will be to me ahead of time. Coaches should inform me if they cannot attend practice. It makes it very difficult to conduct a practice if a coach either communicates late or doesn't let me know at all that they will not be there. Yes, life happens, and sometimes things come up last minute, but it should be the exception, not the norm. Coaches need to inform me ahead of time if they are going to miss practice.

Communication

Frequent communication is another major expectation I have for the staff. In the world of cell phones and the internet, keeping in constant contact with the staff is easier than ever. I will send out text messages and emails and share Google sheets, slides, and docs to communicate with the staff. Coaches need to review any material I share. They need to respond to any texts or email messages that require acknowledgment, answers to questions I have sent, or information. The more I communicate with the staff and keep them in the know, the better we all stay connected, in alignment, and informed.

Mentally ready

When coaches arrive at practice, I expect them to be mentally prepared and ready to work with the players. I urge coaches to set aside any distractions and focus on the task at hand. I know this can be a challenge, but our players deserve to be coached, and it's paramount that the coaches have a rational mind to do this. Being prepared also means that they have a copy of the practice plan and know what is going on that day. Because we share our plans digitally, there is ample time to review them and be mentally prepared for practice.

Building connections

Building connections with the players that go beyond the field is another expectation I have for the staff. I want our coaches to invest in the lives of their players and become a mentor for them. We can only accomplish this when our coaches take the time to talk to the players beyond just coaching them. This can take place before practice, during water breaks, and after practice. I also encourage our coaches to get the players' cell phone numbers so they can send texts or make phone calls as needed. I want the coaches to learn as much about the player's lives as possible. What is their family dynamic? Do they have a girlfriend? Do they have a favorite NFL team? I want our coaches to take the time to find out how the players want to be coached as well. Does yelling at them pump them up, or do they shut down? Do they want to be singled out when they do something right or wrong? How do they want to be praised? I want our players to feel and know that we love them. For me, building relationships with the players is the most important aspect of an assistant coach's job. These are all important pieces of information to know in order to develop that relationship.

On the field coaching

With on-the-field coaching, I expect our coaches to coach every rep that players are involved in. There should not be one play that goes by where a coach is not giving feedback to the players. This is very exhausting and difficult to do, but it must be done. I ask them to make it a "positive sandwich." This means to start with a positive, give constructive feedback (i.e., critique the technique, not the person), and finish it with another positive. We are seeking improvement with each skill we are trying to teach, so it's vital that we provide feedback so the players know exactly what they need to do to improve.

Coaches need to remember that we are teachers, and our classroom is the field. We need to speak in a manner that is clear, concise, and direct without screaming at them. If all we ever do is yell at the players, eventually, they will tune us out, so we need to be selective when we yell. We are human, so sometimes we will get frustrated and blurt out a negative to a player. While this is not what we want, I recognize it happens, so when it does, I ask the coaches to pull the player to the side as soon as possible and talk to him one-on-one. It's important that the player knows that the coach still cares about him and just wants the best out of him. If this isn't possible at the time it happens, we need to make sure we connect with the player before he leaves for the day. We want our players to leave practice feeling good about themselves and know that while we may have jumped on them, we are still in their corner.

There is one area that I expect our coaches to yell at players, and that's when we see a lack of effort. There is no room on the field for players not to give us everything they have in terms of their effort. I expect the coaches to ensure the players meet the required standard. We can tolerate physical mistakes and mental mistakes to a point, but for a lack of effort, the players need to know that this is not acceptable. The only way we know how to do this is to remind them, usually with a loud voice, to give us their best and honest effort when the time calls for it. If effort is lacking, we will stop practicing and do physical activities to refocus. If we have an individual who is a repeat offender, we remove that player from the unit and replace him with another player. We will then talk to the player either during or after practice and let him know that his effort needs to improve, or he will find his reps decreasing in practice. We make it very clear what the expectation is in terms of effort so that all the players know what the standard is.

Once at practice, I expect the coaches to know what drills they are going to do ahead of time. They must get the required equipment and prepare it before working with the position players. This cuts down on wasting time setting up the drill while the players are standing around. Whatever drills are being done, they need to be focused on position-specific techniques and fundamentals. Drills should target the development of the players' position-specific skills. We focus on the skills that will make the players better for their position. I encourage coaches to be creative with their drill selection and setup to get the most out of practice. Coaches often use group drills to increase the number of players and maximize time. This ensures that players are not standing around and are getting plenty of practice doing what they need to do. Any drill that requires more time to explain than execute should not be done. If the drill requires explanation, this needs to take place either in the classroom or before practice begins. With the ability to meet with players via Zoom or Google Meet, this has become increasingly easier to accomplish. Practice time on the field is limited, and every second counts, so the time needs to be treated as sacred.

Be honest and own it.

Sometimes, as coaches, we make mistakes when working with the players. Examples include thinking we saw a player doing something wrong when, in actuality, they did it correctly, teaching a technique that is not correct, explaining a schematic concept that is off-target, or communicating something on an opposing team that is inaccurate.

Whatever the case may be, we are human and make mistakes, but sometimes, our ego prevents us from confessing that we were wrong, especially with the players. This is something our coaches must overcome. When they make a mistake, we ask them to be honest and own it. Let the players know you were wrong, correct it, and move on.

Apologize if your observation was wrong and let the player know they were right. Nothing will damage a relationship with players more than a coach who is unwilling to admit that they were wrong. Players are not dumb, and they see right through this.

When a player asks a question that we don't know the answer to, admit it and let them know you will find out the answer and get back to them. They will respect that a lot more than a coach who just makes something up so that they don't feel inadequate. Again, we have to put our egos in check and own our stuff.

Coach with great enthusiasm

Practice can become boring and pure drudgery to the players if coaches are not diligent in making it fun. Hard work often is not fun. But if the coaches are coaching with energy, passion, and excitement, this can be infectious. The players will feed off of and adopt the coach's personality. If the coaches are lax, speak little, and are apathetic at practice, the players will take that personality on as well. The coaches need to be the spark that ignites the players' enthusiasm for practice.

Years ago, I visited a practice at USC under then-head coach Pete Carroll. As I was observing, I kept hearing and seeing a coach with a thick Southern accent screaming all over the field. He was jumping around, sprinting from one part of the field to the other, and acting like a wild man, but positively. That coach was the former head coach at LSU, Ed Orgeron. This is what I wanted from my coaches. One way to make that happen is to create a competitive environment in practice. Players love to compete, and anything a coach can do to make a drill competitive, the better the players respond and often perform.

Finally, we want our coaches to convince their players, by how they coach, that they are the best position (QB, LB, WR, etc.) coach in America. We want them to make their players feel they are getting the best instruction that any high school player can get. We can only accomplish this if the coach takes his craft seriously and makes the best effort to be that kind of coach.

Language

Communication and speaking are a huge part of the assistant coach's job, and in doing so, we want our coaches to use positive and encouraging language. This means that using profanity, derogatory, and crude speech is unacceptable. I understand that football is a physical sport that requires a certain level of toughness, but that does not mean we need to use profanity to get our point across. As educators, we should use positive language even when we feel frustrated or angry. We suggest our coaches find alternative methods of expression.

Coaches must avoid offensive language about race, ethnicity, religion, socio-economic status, or sexual orientation. We never know every aspect of a player's family. Saying things regarding these areas negatively may affect a player's ability to trust us and know that we have their best interest at heart. Finally, we want to ensure that any language we use is in alignment with our core beliefs. If it is not showing love, we should not be using it.

"You're teaching them to do it or allowing it to happen."

—Dick Tomey.

Several years ago, I was attending a coaches' clinic in San Diego, CA, being run by Coach Bill Williams (see Chapter 1). During one session he was presenting, he quoted the University of Arizona Head Football Coach, Dick Tomey. He said, "You're teaching them to do it or allowing it to happen," regarding what the players you're coaching are doing. This quote has stuck with me over the years, and we have made it one of our coaching themes and mantras. I have made it clear to our coaches that I don't want to hear them tell me they have told a player what they need to do, but they are not getting it done. It doesn't matter how many times you have told a player the correct way to do something. If they are not getting it, it is the coach's fault, not the players, if he repeatedly makes the same mistake over and over. When a player is not doing what you want him to do, then fix it. Give him clearer instructions for additional training. Show him how you want it done, showing him a video of himself or showing him an example (i.e., another player, a video, etc.) of how you want it done. If, after all this, the mistakes continue, find another player, but only after all other avenues have been exhausted. For me, it is more important that a coach takes complete ownership of the player's shortcomings. This needs to be done rather than blame the player for not being able to do what is being asked of him.

WHEN TO LET A COACH GO

It has not happened often in my career as a head coach, but sometimes, assistant coaches need to be let go. More often than not, the coaches who have left our program have done so by their own choice. This happens for a variety of reasons. Changes in life situations, job changes that affect their availability, and a move out of the area are all reasons coaches move on. Attrition of coaches is part of the profession and is always a challenge. Sometimes, the decision for a coach to leave was mutual, simply because it was determined that it would be best for both the program and the coach to depart. In my experience, when this has happened, it has ended positively with no ill feelings (at least on my end).

But sometimes coaches need to be let go for reasons that go beyond their own choice to leave. We should only do this once we have exhausted all other avenues to maintain the coach on staff. As the head coach, you hired that assistant for a reason, so it's your responsibility to train him in the areas of deficiency and get him to do what you need him to do. It's also your job to point out how they can and/or need to improve. Only when the assistant coach cannot show improvement despite training and guidance will they be removed from the staff. Some reasons that we have let coaches go include an inability to positively affect the lives of the young men we are coaching. A failure to get along and effectively work with other members of the staff is another reason. A lack of consistency in doing what is being asked of them is another reason. Last, a personality conflict that does not allow them to be a positive force on the staff is also a contributor.

There are plenty of other reasons that may require letting a coach go, but these are the ones that I have experienced. Again, and I can't stress this enough, it is on you as the head coach to resolve all issues long before you remove someone from your staff. However, once you get to this point, make sure you do so as professionally as possible.

Regardless of the reason, it is always best to keep the departure of the coach as amiable as possible. For me personally, I never wanted a coach leaving our program with any negative feelings about me or the program. I expressed my gratitude, gave them my best wishes, and offered future help.

SUMMARY OF ASSISTANT COACHES

A head coach needs assistants to help them achieve the goals laid out for the program. For me, this meant having coaches who were loyal and cared about the players they were coaching as people first and players second. They need to be prepared each day, work well with others, and want to contribute to something bigger than them. I have been truly blessed by the men who have worked with me, both past and present. It has made my job tremendously easier and more rewarding.

7

WORKING WITH PARENTS: IT TAKES A VILLAGE.

"Coming together is a beginning. Keeping together is progress. Working together is success."

—HENRY FORD

The game itself is great, from Xs and Os to creating practice/game plans to developing new and better ways of coaching. Problems will quickly bury you if you don't plan to develop support. Most of these will have nothing to do with your ability to coach the players. Your program is relational. It's all about the people in your program. You might win some games, even championships. If you don't develop the people in your program, you're missing out on a life-changing opportunity to affect people's lives positively.

There is no shortage of ideas. The challenge is execution. Be honest with yourself about what you can do while maintaining a balance with your family, work (i.e., teaching or off-campus job), health, and personal growth. It all begins with teaching your vision, mission, and core beliefs. This makes up your culture (see Chapter 4) to all the stakeholders in your program, especially your parents. This is not a one-time thing. You must continually reinforce your culture until it becomes second nature to everyone your program touches, most of all your parents. Convince your parents that you have their son's best interest in mind and that you care about them. Then you can do what you want. To gain support from your parents, you must take several steps to show that you care about them and have their son's best interest in mind. Ensure that their sons have a positive, meaningful, and enjoyable experience in your program.

COMMUNICATION

Over the years, I have spoken to literally hundreds of high school head coaches. When I have had the chance to ask them what were some of the biggest challenges they faced, the subject of dealing with parents comes up often. I am always fascinated with not only the topic but why they felt that this was a challenge. I have had issues with parents, but most of the time, they were manageable. Maybe it was these coaches' stories that made little sense to me. Or maybe I was/am naïve, but the parents that I have worked with over the years have been phenomenal. To me, communication has always been a key to successfully working with parents. It must be clear, concise, and effective, as well as frequent. By keeping information constant, it allows everyone to know what is going on. You must try to keep all communication positive. Use as many mediums as possible to keep communication constant: meetings, face-to-face, and phone calls. For emails, texts, or messaging apps, try to use these for communicating information that is generic and applies to everyone. Stay away from using digital communication for any discussions that directly deal with a player. I have always found this type of communication is best face-to-face or over the phone. One tool we have used to keep communication flowing is appointing team representatives at each level. Some programs call it a "team mom." They are a vital source for getting information out to other parents and serving as a buffer between parents and the coaching staff. Our team reps often answer questions and handle matters before I know about them. Clearly communicating expectations reduces parent issues.

Parents and coaches want the same thing for the players: for them to be successful. What success looks like to parents and coaches may be different, but in the end, that's what they both want. Parents want their sons to be loved and treated with respect, to be given an opportunity to play, and to have a great experience. Yes, some parents want more than this. They want their child to be a starter, to play a certain position, or to get a college scholarship, or at least in my experience, this is what most parents want. As long as there is communication, success is achievable.

Finally, in communication, I stress the importance of using our chain of command. So often, especially when there is an issue, parents will go straight to the athletic director, principal, or the district office. They expect the problem to be addressed by someone who has authority over the program. Often, the issue will get kicked back to me for resolution. I ask our parents to bring any issues or concerns that they may have directly to me and allow me the opportunity to resolve them. If I could not resolve the issue, then I ask that they go to our athletic director, then the Assistant Principal in Charge of Athletics, then the principal, and so on. We ask parents to use and respect the chain of command. When they do this, you have a much better chance of resolving issues without involving administration or district personnel.

INVOLVEMENT

I have found over the years that the more you stress to parents to get involved in the program, the better their child's experience will be. Getting involved can take shape in a variety of ways. We begin with a basic premise and offer more opportunities for parents to take part in their child's experience.

The simplest way for parents to get involved with their children is to be present. This could mean showing up for practice. Some coaches have an issue with parents attending practices, but I have never had a problem with it. I like for parents to come out and see the work that their sons are doing. It may provide a better perspective on what their sons are going through. It may also eliminate some issues as to why their sons are not playing when they see them compared to other players. The easiest way to be present is at games. Having someone in the stands who the players know is cheering them on is a significant source of encouragement. I love to see players and their parents after a game. It's a great way for the players to see, know, and feel that their parents love and support them playing.

Another level of involvement is getting parents involved in the booster club. This can take on many forms, but the most basic is to attend meetings. This is a great way for them to stay informed, ask questions, suggest ideas, and look for ways that they can become involved. It may take on the form of working with or leading one of the many committees we have. Special events, fundraising, social media, spirit wear sales, and several others are examples. Some parents decide

Working with Parents: It Takes a Village.

to seek positions on the executive board. They see the value of working in these leadership positions to promote the success of our program. Whether it's becoming our president, vice president, secretary, treasurer, or one of the other board positions makes no difference. Some parents have a genuine gift for doing these jobs and making my life extremely easier.

There are plenty of other opportunities for parents to get involved that are very important to the coaching staff, players, and the program. One major area is feeding the players on game day. We do team meals several hours before kick-off, which requires a lot of coordination and effort. Parents will donate both their time and money to purchase and make food, which is brought on campus before we leave for our game. This is an invaluable activity that benefits both the players and parents who do it. Another job that is essential to our program is game day statistician. It is their job to track and chart all facets of the game as it relates to offense, defense, and special teams. Not only do they take all this information down, but they will also then upload it to a digital platform. This takes a tremendous amount of time and effort. But the parents who have done this for us over the years have provided the coaching staff with valuable information to use as the season moves forward. One job that is vital to the program is team equipment manager. This person oversees all the players' protective equipment and uniforms. It is a daunting task that is critical to the program. Our equipment managers track, maintain, and issue equipment to the players. They also serve as game day repairmen for our players should something happen to their equipment. My job would not be possible without the commitment and hard work of the people who have served in this position. Parents also fill the roles of team photographers, game day filmers, and website managers.

ORGANIZATION

One way to ensure that your parents stay connected and involved is to establish a booster club. When I was hired, the booster club was already in place, so I didn't need to worry about creating one, but we needed to transition it into a 501c3 non-profit organization. I realize that some schools have a booster club that is run through the school's associated student body (ASB). But we found that by creating our own non-profit organization, we could do things faster and easier. It also allows us to have our own tax ID, constitution, bank account, and procedures created by us, which allows for more flexibility. Part of establishing your booster club requires you to have an executive board. They run the meetings and organize events, activities, and committees. Some booster clubs have the head coach as the president. I never felt the need for this because of the competent parents we had in our organization. Our constitution gives me powers to appoint certain positions, which allows me to ensure that I place people in key positions of leadership. The first position I appoint is our president, who is critical to the success of your booster club. This person needs organizational skills and the ability to work well with others. This is especially true because of some of the powerful personalities that inevitably will be a part of the organization. After this, you need a VP, a treasurer, and a secretary. Implementing a registrar is necessary to ensure that all our players are in our system to track their information and donations. Finally, we have team representatives. Each level (Varsity, JV, and Frosh) has its own team rep to ensure we send communication to all our parents. After this, we have several committee positions that are filled by parent volunteers as well.

GENERAL IDEAS

There are plenty of other ways to work with parents and get them to be productive contributors to your program. Try to involve parents in as many non-football decisions as possible. This could take the form of spirit wear sale items, what to eat for team meals, half-time snacks, fundraising ideas, and so on. Giving them the power to make these decisions gives them ownership and allows them to have a voice in areas that don't affect their ability to coach on the field. Another idea is to ask for help in areas that you don't have time to dedicate to yourself. Parent volunteers have done most of the projects and repairs. This includes sleds, trap chutes, weight room projects, water buffalo, golf carts, and equipment that needs welding. Not everyone in your organization enjoys attending meetings and committees. Some parents are great with electrical/mechanical issues and working with their hands. In terms of challenges, try to anticipate potential problems and be active in heading them off. A major part of the job involves hunting out small hot spots and putting them out before they become raging forest fires.

In dealing with issues that arise with players, I deal with them directly and do not involve the parents. Part of the growth process for young men is to allow them to work through the issues that they are having on their own so they can develop the life skill of problem-solving.

Sometimes, this process is hard to accomplish. Many parents today have become accustomed to getting involved anytime their child has a problem (i.e., helicopter parents). If meeting with the player alone is unavoidable and a parent insists on having a meeting face-to-face, I always ask ahead of time what the topic will be. I don't want to be surprised, so I need to know what the issues are so I am prepared.

The bulk of the parent's requests to meet face-to-face have to do with playing time. Parents are clever. They will mask the issue with other things that are not really an issue. They do this so they can meet face-to-face to talk about their sons' playing time and/or the position they are playing. If I feel the issue is about playing time, I will not meet face to face but will deal with it on a phone call. It's usually a quick conversation. It involves me telling the parents to trust the coaching staff and allow us to do what is in the best interest of both the team and the player. If the parent still insists on meeting face-to-face, I will ask the player's position coach, the player, and the parent to be present at the meeting.

The first question I will ask the parent (s) when we sit down to meet is what they would like the outcome to be once the meeting is over. This gets right to the point and core of why we are meeting. Sure, some parents will dance around the issue of playing time, bringing up other areas of concern. But inevitably, it usually works its way back to playing time. Once it does, I will either reference our phone conversation or have the position coach speak about the player's lack of playing time. In my experience, most of the time. The player knows why they are not getting as much playing time and will be on your side, defending your decision to their parents. It becomes very clear quickly that the issue is not something that the player has a problem with, but the parent does. Once we get down to it, I believe it's best to be honest with the parents and the player. Let them know why they are not getting as much playing time and what they can do to improve their opportunities to play. This usually benefits you, and everyone leaves at least feeling heard.

If the issue is something more serious and does not involve playing time, I will usually handle it with a phone call. If that doesn't help, I'll meet with the parent (s) with an assistant coach, athletic director, or administrator present. I want to ensure that I am covered and have a witness to anything that is shared or said while in the meeting. The topics vary. Bullying, coaching issues, academics, drugs/alcohol,

Working with Parents: It Takes a Village.

and family concerns could all be factors. I try to support the parents and let them know I am here to help in any way possible. Sometimes, the parents communicate to me that the only thing that their child is concerned about is playing football. As a result, they will try to leverage this by telling the child that if they don't "toe the line," they will take football away. I rarely support this method of bargaining with the players. But in some extreme cases, this may be the only thing left to get the child to either do or not do what they are supposed to be doing.

ROLE OF THE PARENT

Each spring, before the start of spring practice, I will go over all this information in a parent meeting. Once I have covered these areas, as well as others, I will then go over the roles and responsibilities of the players. Following this, I will go over the role and steps to being a winning parent.

In a winning organization, I ask them to be their child's biggest fan by loving them unconditionally and supporting them. I remind parents that their support should never be about the quality of their performance. Their child's participation should never be a contractual agreement where they must produce to be loved and supported. So many times, parents will withhold love or affection from their child because they did not perform up to their expectations during practice or a game. I remind them that all their children want is to be loved, encouraged, and supported while they play the game they love.

As mentioned previously, I ask them to be present at all team-related events, activities, and functions in which they can attend, as well as all games. Just being there is often enough for the players to feel supported.

Finally, I remind parents to support the coach's decisions both on and off the field. When they are home with their child, they need to keep their opinions and feelings to themselves. This is especially true as it relates to any decisions the coaching staff has made regarding any aspect of the team. This could involve playing time and positions being played. It could be the scheme of the offense or defense. It could be any other on-the-field decision the coaching staff has made. During games, we ask our parents, as hard as it may be, to support the players. We ask that they not yell "suggestions" or criticisms of what the coaching staff should or should not be doing during the game.

Once I have gone over these basic concepts, I will go into greater detail on how parents are to be winning parents. I provide them with several steps that they should try their best to execute. First, I remind parents that competition is a good thing and that their child will benefit from it, not only against other players but against themselves. We stress to parents that we want them to support their children as they attempt to improve themselves against the best version of themselves. By doing this, the parents reinforce what the coaches are trying to teach the players.

Second, we ask our parents not to define success by winning or losing, which clouds what we are trying to teach the players. We want our players to give their best effort in all they do, which is our definition of success. While winning is important and a desired outcome, it is not how we define success.

Third, we ask our parents not to "coach" their children. Parents will offer "suggestions" and advice to their children on what they can do to improve their technique, skills, or playing time. Often, it is unsolicited. Kids don't want to hear that from their parents unless they ask for it. This is especially true after a hard-fought game where either the player did not perform well or the team lost. As hard as it is, we ask our parents to be just that: a parent. We will remind parents it's their child's experience, not theirs. A parent's job is to make the sport fun by supporting their child and not coaching them.

Fourth, we ask parents to remember to love their children unconditionally for who they are, not what they do or perform. They often express love for kids through their performance in practice or a game. This can be very straining and even damaging to the parent-child relationship. We ask our parents to remember the importance of self-esteem in all their interactions with their children. Words are powerful and can do a lot of damage if not delivered in the right way. In the end, we want our parents to understand the importance of loving up their children, regardless of how well they perform.

Fifth, we ask parents to give their children the gift of failure. This can be the most challenging for some folks. So many times, parents don't want their children to feel pain, hurt, or frustration. By soothing the child, they don't allow them to experience failure and how to cope with it. This can be very damaging to the development of young players' growth and maturity if they don't learn how to deal with failure. Failure is not a negative thing unless we make it a negative thing. Failure is an opportunity to grow. It allows us to see what we did wrong, learn from it, apply the lessons learned, and improve. Instead of not allowing the child to experience failure, we encourage parents to challenge them to try harder. This can be done when parents stress the process rather than the outcome. By doing this, failure becomes an outstanding teacher that can lead us to our goals. Ultimately, we want the players in our program to learn and grow from failure, and parents need to help in that process.

Sixth, we ask parents to avoid comparisons and respect developmental differences that they see with other players. One of the common challenges we see in parents is their desire to compare their child to another and try to get their child to be like others. This is a recipe for disaster. We ask the parents to focus on their child's development, considering where they are currently. Some players are bigger, stronger, and faster than others. Parents need to respect the differences to avoid comparing their children to others.

Finally, we ask parents to help their children keep a perspective on the sports experience. Children need to learn that playing sports is about learning, growing, and challenging themselves. This means going beyond their normal comfort zone. Yes, competing to win is important, but that's not the end game. We want players to keep a healthy perspective on why they are playing. They should enjoy the experience, have fun competing, love being with their teammates, and find a sense of fulfillment in the effort they are giving. This is a great opportunity for parents to teach that to their children.

WINNING, COMPETITION, AND PLAYING TIME

I am a competitor by nature, as are most coaches. I love the preparation and the event of competing against a worthy opponent. Whether it's coaching a football game or playing Monopoly with my own children, I want to win. It is VERY important to me, and I am going to do whatever it takes to either put our team or myself in a position that gives us/me the best opportunity to win. But winning is not the only reason I coach. Is it important to me? Yes. But as I've tried to articulate throughout this book up to now, it's not my sole reason for coaching. It is paramount that I get this point across to our parents. I want them to understand that while winning is important to me, I have a dual purpose in why I coach.

I am coaching the players in our program to teach life skills and character, improve their growth and self-esteem, and promote teamwork. This also involves teaching how to be an excellent role model for younger players, fair play, and integrity. We also teach how to play the game with proper technique and fundamentals. If we are successful in doing all of this, we will be a winner. With all of this, we ultimately have to teach the players and parents what a winner looks like.

In our program, we define a winner as someone who is a team player. They care about their teammates more than themselves. This means that they respect and value not only their teammates but the opponent as well. They will put the team's interests and welfare before their own. They will help their teammates. A winner is a hard worker who understands the value of the process and pushes themselves outside their comfort zone to improve and get better. They are a good sport and value the rules of the game. They are positive leaders who actively seek ways to guide and help their teammates. We want them to take responsibility for their actions and take winning and losing in stride.

They need to be coachable and listen to feedback, be honest and dependable, and, regardless of the situation, display a winning attitude. When a player can do all this, it makes a coach's job easy. We must explain this to parents so they can help their child show what a winner looks and acts like.

With competition, the game dictates that we play against somebody, but ultimately, the game is an opportunity for us to show the best version of ourselves. We stress that while the game requires us to play against an opponent, they are not the enemy. We don't use those terms when describing teams that we play against. They are simply the test placed in front of us to determine if we are willing and able to give our best. Games should never be a life-or-death struggle. There are too many real-life events happening in our world today to compare a game to that. It should be all about us testing our preparation against a worthy opponent to see if we can accomplish what we have worked so hard to do. Parents must understand this and reinforce it to their children so that when games are being played, they keep a healthy perspective.

The last thing I will talk to parents about involves how playing time is determined. I save this for last because I want parents to know all the other things we outline with them are what's most important to me. We determine playing time by several factors. One is meeting, training, and practice attendance. They need to know that players who miss these sessions consistently will not learn what they need to learn to be successful. The second is attitude and effort. If their child shows up with a great attitude and displays relentless effort, this will increase their child's ability to get on the field. Finally, talent and ability will assess who gets on the field and who does not. One is not more important than the other. We have had plenty of very talented players who played very little for us because they missed practice or displayed a poor attitude. Conversely, we have had players who showed up every day and gave a great effort, but their skill set was such that it was difficult for them to crack the starting lineup. We must weigh these carefully to put the best players on the field and give us the best chance to succeed.

DEALING WITH THE "1%ERS"

No matter how hard you try to do all the things outlined in this chapter, you invariably will have parents who just don't see or share your vision. As a result, they will undermine all that you are trying to do to run a successful program and develop their sons. They won't get on board and will look for others who feel the same. I call these parents the

"1%ers" because they are the ones that can make a coach's job extremely difficult. In the end, you must remain faithful to yourself and what you are doing as a coach and trust that what you and your staff are doing is the right thing to do. When we experience parents like this, we try our best to share with them our vision, mission, and purpose for doing what we do. One of two things happens. They accept it and, at the bare minimum, discontinue their complaining and simply support their sons. Or they take their son out of our program and sometimes transfer schools. While the latter can be disheartening, you must accept the fact that some folks, no matter how hard you try, just are not happy with your program. It is at this point that you have to move on both mentally and emotionally. The one thing I have learned in dealing with the "1%ers" is that most of the time, their sons were doing fine in our program. With a little more grit, toughness, and hard work, they would have eventually had a great experience in our program. If only their parents would have just sat back and allowed the process to take place. But the world has made this extremely difficult for parents to do. Players have quit or transferred to another program because of dissatisfaction. While this is not something that I will ever be OK with, it is the reality of coaching that I have had to accept.

SUMMARY OF WORKING WITH PARENTS

Parents can be your greatest asset or your worst nightmare, depending on how you incorporate them into your program. I have always found parents to be a tremendous help in our program and in the development of the players we coach. They are a great resource for so many reasons that it would be foolish not to tap into them and make them your ally. In the end, the parents want the same thing that we, as coaches, want, and that is for their children to be successful.

8

LEADERSHIP PRINCIPLES: WHAT IT TAKES TO LEAD AS A COACH AND PLAYER

*"Good leaders don't make excuses.
Instead, they figure out a way to get things done."*

–Jocko Willink

Leadership. What exactly does it mean? Some have attempted to define it in simple terms, while others have used complex diagrams, formulas, and algorithms to explain it. A recent survey found that there are over

15,000 books on the subject if you search for them at a bookstore or library. What we know about leadership is that it is a critical component of any family, team, organization, company, or nation. It is the one area that can separate one from others, both positively and negatively. It has a variety of components and applications that require a certain level of skill in order for it to be effective. If done correctly, it can make all the difference, positively, to make your team the best version of itself.

Over the years, I have compiled a sizable library of books, many of which discuss leadership. I have read books on leadership from many sources, such as business leaders, military leaders, and coaches. My goal was to narrow down the definition into one simple concept and idea. The issue, however, is that it's not that simple. There are so many takes, approaches, definitions, applications, and concepts it became a struggle for me to pinpoint one simple message. So, rather than rack my brain trying to do so, I synthesized all the material I was reading. I would take the best of the best and melt it into my version of what I thought leadership should look like. I looked into different leaders to find what would work for me, and I avoided mistakes that were made. With each passing year, I built different ideas into my leadership style that I felt were essential to my growth as a leader. What is critical to know and understand is that leadership development is a never-ending cycle of growth. While your core tenets may remain the same, you need to adapt and adjust along the way, paying close attention to the people you lead. Stay relevant and effective by continuing to learn and grow. As best as I can summarize it in the simplest terms, leadership is influence. You can take all the different components that make up being a leader and influence others to do what you want them to do.

LEADERSHIP PRINCIPLES THAT I THINK ARE ESSENTIAL

Throughout my career, I have learned a lot about leadership from a variety of sources (books, speakers, videos, etc.). Still, by far, the most important element of being a leader is being true to oneself. You must be your real self. I have been guilty of reading about someone in a leadership position and attempting to apply that same model to my situation, only to fail miserably. My mistake was trying to be someone else, someone who I could never possibly emulate, because my personality would not allow it. If you're a passionate person, trying to be stoic and thoughtful, while definitely applicable, it will be a losing battle. You will become frustrated and feel trapped as you try to be something you're not. If you're passionate, harness it and use it to your benefit. Temper your passion and funnel it positively. That allows you to be a passionate leader. If you're naturally quiet, being loud can make you feel uncomfortable. Whatever your temperament is, mold your leadership style around that and be yourself.

Next, being honest with yourself and those you lead is critical. Nothing will cause you to lose credibility faster with those you lead than not being truthful. As uncomfortable as it may be, you must be honest about everything you are attempting to do. Own up to mistakes. Communicate your observations, thoughts, and feelings, but do so without being hurtful. No matter how discreet, someone's feelings may still get hurt, but the truth is always best. It allows you to have a clear conscience and know that you have expressed the truth, regardless of the situation.

Being humble is also an essential part of leadership. You must accept you do not have all the answers and will learn from others. Humility in leadership signals a lack of ego, an ability to admit wrongdoing, and receptiveness to others' views. You make others comfortable when you don't pretend to know everything and use others' ideas. Being humble creates an environment where everyone feels they are a part of the decision-making process and what they have to say matters.

To be an effective leader, you need to show the people you lead you care about them as people, not what they can do for you. Often, people in leadership positions make decisions that benefit them at the expense of others. We refer to this as *transactional leadership*. While in the short run, you may get what you want, over time, this type of leadership is not sustainable. It will build resentment with those you lead and causes them to no longer do what you want them to do. People want to know that you care about them beyond what they can provide for you. This means you need to get to know them, listen to them and their concerns, give advice and direction that will help them, and ultimately serve their needs. Once people know you genuinely care about them as people, there really isn't anything they won't do for you when asked. This is often called *transformational leadership* or servant leadership. By serving the needs of others, it builds a solid foundation of trust and support from those you are leading. Fulfilling the needs of those in your organization doesn't mean you give them all they ask for, but you are working to help them reach their full potential.

Jocko Willink and Leif Babin share core principles of leadership in their book *Extreme Ownership*. Leaders take full responsibility for their command. This means that no matter what happens, as a leader, you don't make excuses for why things happen. You don't blame others, and you don't deflect responsibility. When you have done all you can to explain and prepare your organization, yet the task remains undone, it can be especially challenging. If this happens, it's because your explanations weren't clear enough, or you didn't remove someone from a task they weren't qualified for. In the end, extreme ownership does

Leadership Principles: What It Takes to Lead as a Coach and Player

not allow you to make excuses for why things did not get done. Ultimately, everything within your organization falls on you. When you lead, you take responsibility and ensure everyone knows what to do.

One of the most important aspects of being a leader is to lead by example. You set the tone for how things are going to be done. You cannot expect those you lead to do what you are asking them to do if you are not willing to do it. If you're asking them to work hard, put the work in yourself so that others feel a sense of obligation to do it themselves if, for no other reason, they see you doing the same. When responding to adversity, you must keep a level demeanor if you expect those you lead to do the same. If you lose control of your emotions each time something goes wrong, how can you expect those around you not to do the same? By doing the little things that are often required of being a coach, you have to do them yourself if you want others to do the same. The list goes on and on, but the principle remains the same. You must lead by example so that others will follow suit.

Finally, if you want to be an effective leader, you need to focus on the areas and things that are within your control. You cannot get distracted or frustrated over things that you have zero influence or control over. While this can be very difficult to navigate, remind yourself to focus on the controllable events in your life. This requires a tremendous amount of discipline, but it is essential to remain an effective leader.

We stress the importance of the equation $E+R=O$ (Event + Response = Outcome), which comes from Tim and Brian Kight of Focus 3. The only part of that equation that we have complete control over is our response. We stress to our players that our response, referred to as the R Factor, is the only thing that matters because it's within our control. To do this, you need to exercise a three-step process: think, feel, and act. In order to think, you need to press pause so you can get your emotions under control and gain clarity over the situation. Next, you need to honor how you feel and get your mind right so you can decide on how to respond. Finally, you need to step up and act. It's really that simple. By using this method, you can gain better control over focusing on the things that matter most and are within your control.

Another formula we like to use is the OODA (pronounced ooo-Duh; It stands for Observe, Orient, Decide, Act.) loop, created by the former U.S. Air Force fighter pilot John Boyd. It helped fighter pilots deal with stressful and chaotic situations while in combat. But we can use the principles for any situation. By applying this formula, much like the R factor, one can make a stressful situation much more manageable. It will help you gain control over a situation that may seem out of your control. In the end, the best leaders are the ones who focus on what they are in control of.

LEADING AS A COACH

Regardless of whether you are the head coach or an assistant, it is your responsibility to lead your players. You do this by doing all the above and getting your players to do what you want them to do. Whether it is behaving as a respectful student in the classroom or defending a slant route, what the players do ultimately falls on you. Players may not always follow what we expect, but it's our job to help guide them. We must communicate the standards we expect our players to follow, regardless of the area, and hold them accountable. We must do this consistently and effectively. Most players want this type of structure, so it typically benefits us, but sometimes, they will need to be reminded. As a coach, it is important that we understand and never grow tired of leading them to do what needs to be done.

Leadership Principles: What It Takes to Lead as a Coach and Player

Part of our job as coaches is to train our players on how to be leaders. I wish I had a simple answer on how to do this, but the fact is, I have experimented with a variety of ways, some that have worked and some that have not. There is no one right way to train your players on how to be a leader, as each year of players is different.

Sometimes, players naturally gravitated towards a leader, while in other years, there was no leader. Whichever is the case, it's your job as a coach to develop them.

A challenge I have observed is the absence of youth playing in the neighborhood without adult involvement. As a kid, when we played, regardless of the game, we picked the teams, we made up the rules, and we enforced the game. There were no adults around to manage infractions, ensure that everyone played fairly, or handle disputes that often erupted. That fell squarely on our shoulders. Naturally, as we grew older and started playing high school sports, we were a self-regulating group of athletes. The coaches managed the teams, but the players handled the drama. We were self-made leaders and took that role seriously. It is uncommon to find players who have not had adults overseeing their sporting experiences from an early age. Many young people today are lacking in leadership skills due to not playing outside without adult supervision. As a result, they rely on adults for instruction in high school. This makes it that much more difficult to break the cycle of relying on adults to have all the answers and address any issues that arise.

To address this, each year I have been the head coach, I have tried to train our players to be leaders in the off-season. Each January, I meet weekly with players who show leadership potential until spring practice. In some years, this has been only senior players, while in other years, I have had all grade levels present. I have identified certain players as potential leaders but also allowed anyone to take part in the training.

This has been the most productive method because it gives anyone a chance to be a leader. I stress to the team that we will select our team captains from the players who attend these weekly meetings. This has been a good way to ensure that anyone who has a desire to be a captain attends these meetings.

I have used a variety of materials with the players in these meetings. Some years, I have used books (too many solid ones to list), while in other years, I have used different articles or portions of unique books to train them. Regardless of what you use, anything that gets the players to think and discuss what it means to be a leader will be beneficial. My goal with these training sessions is to get our players prepared and ready to be the voice of the team and lead the other players throughout the season.

To facilitate training the leaders of our program, we created cohorts (or squads) where we placed a leader, usually a senior, over a group of players. The number of cohorts we have created depends on the season and the number of players in our program. But the basic premise is that we have a player leading a small group of other players. I will select *Centurions* or squad leaders, and they will draft the other players. They will select an assistant, called an *Optio*, to be their number two in charge of the cohort. The rest of the cohort members are called *Legionnaires*.

By placing all our players in cohorts, it serves several purposes. It creates a communication tree to spread information. It also provides an opportunity for any player on the team to bring up issues or concerns for their leader. They will either attempt to address them or bring them to my attention. We will also do competitions between one cohort and another, attempting to strengthen cohort unity and teamwork. There are a lot of programs that offer rewards for things like attendance, grades, and community service, but I haven't found one that's easy to manage. If you have a coach on your staff who would create and take on this task, do it. It is a great way to create competition and player-to-player accountability. For us, using this formula of creating cohorts has been helpful in giving our players an opportunity to serve and learn how to be leaders in our program.

Finally, another idea we have employed is our leadership council. This consists of players from each grade level who players and coaches select to serve on the council. This has been useful, providing players with a say in our program and letting me know what's happening.

LEADING AS A PLAYER

When training our players to lead their teammates, there are several characteristics they must show to influence and lead. The most important thing that our leaders must do is work harder than anyone else on the team. They must work hard in the weight room, completing all sets and reps correctly with the right weight. They set the tone in the weight room by showing their teammates how it is supposed to be done with a no-nonsense attitude and approach to training. On the practice field, they need to strive their hardest to outwork everyone else who plays their position and anyone else on the field. If doing sprints, they need to try to be first or, at the very least, strain to the finish. If we are doing a team period, they need to finish every play through the whistle.

Regardless of the assigned activity on the field, your leaders need to be the hardest workers on the team, period. If they are not, they cannot be effective leaders. The rest of the team will not respect them.

The next most important thing you need to train your leaders to be is vocal. This does not mean they are screamers in the weight room or at practice. Will they, at times, need to do that? Of course. But that should be the exception, not the norm. When I say vocal, I mean they need to speak to their teammates. They need to talk to them, both on and off the training field. Just being a good example is not enough to be an effective leader. They need to talk, and they need to do it often. This communication is not random.

Have a goal in mind when doing it, such as creating connections or relaying info. For some players, this can be a real challenge, as they are shy or lack confidence in speaking to their peers. It's your job as the coach to help them overcome this because your leaders have to be vocal to be effective.

Your leaders must be good followers as well. They must be able to take instructions from the coaching staff and provide a positive example to the rest of the team on how to follow. Whether it is technique or how to behave, they must show an ability to execute what we ask of them. Their teammates will have seen their example as productive followers, which will help them when they lead others.

Players must address and overcome challenges to lead their teammates. By far, the biggest internal hurdle your leaders need to overcome is the fear of losing friends because we have placed them in a leadership position. In speaking to our players during our leadership training sessions, this concern comes up more than any other. We work hard to train them that leading their peers will not cause them to lose friends as long as they develop relationships with them. Building relationships with teammates makes accountability easier. Leaders are afraid of alienating friends on the team. We stress the importance of laying a solid foundation before it ever gets to that point. We want our leaders to influence their friends on the team to do what needs to be done in the best interest of the team using the "carrot rather than the stick" method. Our leaders need to learn how to cultivate strong relationships. Listening to their friends, investing in them, and being helpful are all integral. This will build leadership capital with their friends and teammates.

At times, student leaders have difficulty getting their teammates to comply with their requests. When other players blow them off, ignore them, or are just plain deviant, this is a clear sign that there is a lack of respect for them as leaders. We challenge our leaders to ask themselves why that is. Is it because they have not invested enough time in the other players? Maybe they are yelling at them instead of talking to them. Is it just that the other players don't feel any need to listen to or do what is being asked of them by one of their peers? Whatever the case may be, just like when they are concerned with losing friends, we encourage our leaders to invest time and energy into their teammates. Show them they genuinely care about them as people first, teammates second. By doing this, they create an environment in which their teammates will come to respect them and be more willing to do what is being asked of them.

Another hurdle that must be overcome is a lack of confidence from your team leaders. Some may feel inadequate to lead and hide in the shadows, blending in with peers and avoiding their responsibilities. It is our job as coaches to provide support, encouragement, and guidance to our team leaders so that they can do what we need them to do with confidence. You can do this by supporting them publicly in front of the team and correcting them privately away from others so as not to undermine them with their peers. Being a leader for many of these young players does not come naturally, and it is not uncommon for them to doubt and question their own abilities. It is our job to build them up, give them the confidence and skills they need, and support them in leadership roles.

There are several other areas that your team leaders must show to be effective leaders for their teammates. They must attend all practices, training sessions, and team functions. It's nearly impossible to have influence if they are not present and find ways to not be with the team. They need to listen and follow all team rules to ensure that their peers are seeing them tow the company line. Team leaders need to be "coachable" and open to constructive feedback not only from the coaches but also from their peers. They need to lead with a sense of humility. This shows their teammates that they are human, infallible, and willing to learn from anyone. They need to put the team's needs before their own, which requires a tremendous level of unselfishness. They may encounter situations where they have to carry out tasks they are not willing to do. But if they really care about the team above themselves, they will do so without hesitation. They need to do whatever is asked of them in a sincere, honest manner, demonstrating their best ability in doing so by being positive and having a great attitude.

Our team leaders should show the behavior we expect from the other players. They need to speak to their teammates with positive and encouraging language so that their peers see they care about them and want what's best for them. They need to keep their academics in order and make sure they are doing what they are supposed to be doing in the classroom. This goes a long way in showing their peers that being a student first is a top priority for the team. They must behave responsibly and not become a burden to the program when away from the team or campus. Last, they need to show a level of maturity with their emotions and not lose control when things are not going well. They need to ensure that they are not whining, complaining, or making excuses regarding anything that happens with the team.

Your team leaders must learn all these things equally, and you must constantly reinforce them with them. Going over it one time and moving on will not lead to effective team leaders. Just like any other skill being taught, coaches must ensure that leadership training is an ongoing process, drilled daily.

SUMMARY OF LEADERSHIP

Leadership is influence. How you, as a coach, do it and how you train your players is entirely up to you. There is no one-size-fits-all-all, and you must be mindful of how you lead the people within your program. Don't be afraid to try all methods to train and lead your people. Leadership is a dynamic concept that requires constant upkeep, learning, and application. The more you talk about it, demonstrate it, and maintain it, the better you and everyone in your program will become in leadership.

9

WINNING THE WRONG WAY: WHAT'S REALLY IMPORTANT FOR COACHING

"There are a lot of teams who win and do it the wrong way."

—COACH LADOUCEUR,
FORMER HEAD FOOTBALL COACH, DE LA SALLE HS, CA

As mentioned in Chapter 1, early in my career, I would meet with legendary Coach Ladouceur of De La Salle High School (CA) while attending a coaching clinic. When we sat down to talk, he made a statement that really stuck with me all these years later. He said, "There are a lot of teams out there who win and do it the wrong way." I wasn't really sure what he meant by that, but throughout my career, I have gained a much better understanding of what exactly he meant by it. It has really shaped the "why" in terms of my coaching career.

When I first became the head coach at Saugus, I was very concerned with simply winning on the scoreboard, regardless of the cost. This meant I said and did things that were not in the best interest of my family, the school, and the players. It's not that I didn't care about the players I coached, but sometimes I put winning above what I knew was the right thing to do. As time passed and my experience progressed, I learned to really focus on what matters most for coaching the young men.

BUILDING RELATIONSHIPS

The biggest thing I have learned over the years is that it's all about relationships. Life is relational, and building and maintaining relationships must be the single most important part of your job as a coach. This, of course, starts with the players. They must be your top priority, and you have to work on strengthening that relationship every day.

Regardless of your personality, you must do all that you can to show the players you genuinely care about them as people long before you care about them as players. This means investing in them and getting to know them on a deeper level. There is no one way to do this, but it must be done. It can be something as simple as talking to them before practice, during stretching, or after practice. It could be while they are in your classes or in between classes. Before player meetings, you can call on a couple of players and ask simple questions about them before you start. You can fire off a text message just to check in with them. Some coaches have their players fill out a questionnaire so they can get information that goes a little deeper. Whatever methods you use, what matters most is getting to know the player on a much more personal level.

Another technique is to tell the players about you and your life experiences. Players look at their coaches as this higher power. They couldn't possibly understand or relate to anything that they have or are currently going through. Sharing your life story with them allows them behind the curtain and shows them you're human. I have found over the years that the more I open up and share my life experiences with the players, the easier it becomes for them to do the same. Prioritize relationships to make your program unforgettable.

With the adults associated with your program, this has to be done as well. Taking the time to get to know your program's support people and show them they are important is vital. You want these people to feel connected to your program and feel that it's their program as well. There is nothing revolutionary about what you need to do to get them to feel this way. Talk to them. Ask them about their lives, their families, their jobs, or anything else that is important to them. Over the years, I have discovered that most people love to share about their lives and are more than willing to talk with you if you make the effort.

For other people who may not be directly involved with your program on your campus but whose support you would love to have, take the time to invest in them as well. The head custodian and principal's secretary are the two most important people on any campus. I have made sure that I take care of both folks on our campus. Talking with them, giving them football shirts or hats, and just simply thanking them for all the hard work they do on our campus is something I did. With teachers, campus security, or any other campus employees, I attempt to say hello and spend a few minutes talking to them whenever I get a chance. I want everyone to know that I am just like them, a human being who is there to serve the students. I work hard to build these relationships because I want everyone whom I come in contact with to feel that we are all in this together.

Finally, when talking with people out in the community, I talk to anyone who either talks to me about our school or who may have a connection with our program. Sometimes, it's parents or players of other school programs, alums who graduated, or someone who noticed our school logo. Regardless of the reason, I make the time and put in the effort to speak to people who have expressed an interest in our school or program. I aim for people to remember our conversation positively and share it with others.

MAINTAINING RELATIONSHIPS BEYOND HIGH SCHOOL

Once our players have completed playing for us and graduated from high school, we have found that the relationship between us continues. It is not uncommon for players to come and visit us either at school during the day or at practice. Many times, they come by just to say hello and see how the team is doing. Other times, they may come by seeking advice on life issues. Whatever the case may be, maintaining that relationship beyond high school is a valuable part of the complete experience.

It is our role to continue to guide these young people as long as they continue to seek our advice and counsel. Players will call, text, email, or come by in person asking for all kinds of advice on a variety of topics. I have aided players in making college, career, and life decisions. It doesn't matter what the issue is or what they want to talk about; it's our duty to make the time to talk with them and continue to provide guidance. Outside of their parents, we usually are the most influential person who players have in their lives. That does not end when they leave our program. It simply adapts and takes on a different appearance. We owe that to our players. It's a lifelong process and commitment to our players to be there for them, much like a parent is to a child.

TEACHING LIFE LESSONS

While football is a passion and love of mine, it is a vehicle that I use to teach life lessons. Yes, we want to win football games, but it's the ability to affect lives for years to come that really drives what we do. The love of the game attracts the players to come, which means we have a captive audience. They may not know it, but the players are being given invaluable life lessons on how to be an outstanding person for the rest of their lives. Our goal is for our players to remember the lessons we have taught them and use them throughout their lives. Like a parent, we teach and equip them for a life of success, but ultimately, they have to choose to live that life.

How to treat others

Besides what we have already discussed, we focus on other topics as well. As one of our core beliefs states, an unconquerable character means we love people, but it's how to do that consistently that we must stress. We want our players to value other people because they are human beings. Everyone matters and deserves to be treated with respect. We ask our players to talk to other students on our campus, whether at brunch, lunch or in their classes, who they might not normally talk to. We want them to get comfortable interacting with as many people as possible because it benefits both parties. When walking around campus, we ask our players to say hello to students they see sitting by themselves. This is especially important in today's world, where so many young people feel isolated and alone as if no one sees them. We want our players to be the catalyst of change on our campus, really get to know as many people as possible, and be the leaders on our campus.

We stress the importance of getting to know others and accepting those with different opinions than ours. People are quick to judge without fully understanding. Our culture, which has become so dependent on social media, is quick to attack those who differ from us. This platform allows for anonymous, hateful, and false speech with no repercussions. Our players need to be the opposite of this. We want them to accept what makes them different from others and take it one step further by appreciating those differences. It may be someone who looks different from us based on race, hair color, fashion, or any other outward appearance. Or someone who practices a different religion than our own or doesn't practice one at all, or someone who has a different sexual orientation than our own. We want our players to accept others for who they are, period. This, however, does not end with just acceptance. We want our players to learn to appreciate their differences and get to know others on a deeper level. This doesn't mean we expect our players to be best friends with everyone they meet. But it means taking that step to go a little beyond just acknowledging other people. We want them to treat everyone, regardless of who they are or what they believe, how they would like to be treated. Our world needs more people like this who can look beyond differences and truly accept others for who they are.

Being a good person

You would think that this idea of being a good person would be simple for most people, but my experience has shown that it is not. The whole idea of being a good person is subjective. Who says what is good for one person is wrong for another? There are varying degrees by which a group of people defines what it means to be a good person. When I talk about being a good person, I describe very specific behaviors that most people on the planet can agree on, leaving little room for subjectivity. For the sake of not being redundant, the following characteristics apply to players, coaches, parents, or anyone else who is a part of our program.

HONESTY AND INTEGRITY

When I talk about being a good person, the first thing we discuss with our players is being someone who shows honesty and integrity. Today, many young people have a hazy understanding of what it means to be truthful. Our society has done an amazing job of blurring the lines between what is honest and what is not. We stress the idea of not lying or bending the truth so that there is no misunderstanding of what is going on. We expect everyone who is a part of our organization to show integrity, which, simply defined, means doing what is right when no one else is looking. This can be challenging, especially for young people, who have a variety of opportunities to do things they should not be doing and get away with it. We stress to our players that you can fake it, lie, cheat, or be dishonest, and you may get away with it in the short run, but eventually, it will catch up with you. Rather than put themselves in that situation, we work hard to ensure our players are honest and live with integrity.

KINDNESS AND POLITENESS

We want to be known as people who are kind and polite to those we encounter. This may sound contradictory in a game that promotes aggressiveness, toughness, and a no-mercy attitude. But our players must understand that even in the game of football, there is a place for kindness, both on and off the field. We preach to our players to respect differences and embrace everyone with the mindset that they are human beings, just like us. There are enough people who are mean and intolerant towards others without us contributing to it. You can play the game aggressively and still show kindness. We do this by helping our opponent up after a play or complimenting them if they are doing something well. Doing this takes nothing away from us trying to be dominant on the field, but it shows a sense of compassion for the opposing team.

Having manners and being polite is another area we stress to the players. We want people who meet our players to walk away thinking that they are respectable young men. We accomplish this by stressing to our players to say "please" and "thank you" as often as possible. This may sound like common sense, but players come from all walks of life, and sometimes, this may not be part of their upbringing, so it is our job to remind them. We emphasize to them that even when they're not in uniform, people may recognize them as part of our football program. People often tell me about the positive impression our players make with their politeness. When this happens, you know you're doing something right. We have gotten emails or messages from community members who have said the opposite as well. It is our job to teach and train our players to be respectful, demonstrate manners, and be polite wherever they go.

SELFLESSNESS

One of the more challenging qualities to teach our players is having an attitude of unselfishness. In a world that constantly preaches a mindset of "what's in it for me" or "I'm going to get what's rightfully mine," this is one of the biggest battles we face. People are selfish by nature, which, at times, we need to be, but there are plenty of examples where this need not be the case. We need to use discernment to know when to be selfish and when not to be. We urge our players to look after themselves while being mindful of how their behavior affects others. One of the quickest ways to destroy a team is having players who only care about themselves. This could be due to playing time, their stats, or the recognition they feel they deserve. We stress to them to be mindful of their heart and to truly seek the meaning behind why they do what they do. Is it for what is best for them, or is it for what is best for the team? We ask them to be aware of what they say and do to ensure that it is coming from a genuine place of concern for others.

OTHER AREAS OF IMPORTANCE THAT PLAYERS NEED TO KNOW

There are other areas of the players' lives we talk about and address to make them aware of their surroundings. The language they speak and the choices they make can have a devastating impact on themselves and others if they are not mindful.

How the players treat women is a constant topic of discussion. We remind our players that everyone deserves to be treated with respect and love, but women need to be treated with special reverence. This does not mean that we look down on women or think less of them. But in a society that exploits women for our (i.e., men's) pleasure or benefit, we want our players to have a different perspective. We remind our players that all women are someone else's mother, sister, or valuable member of their respective family. They deserve to be treated equally and as if they are part of our own family. We educate our players on why derogatory language is inappropriate. Many are completely clueless that some of the speech they use is inappropriate or offensive to women. They hear this language used in the music they listen to, the movies they watch, or the things they see on social media. Many of them simply don't know that this language is unacceptable.

With dating, we talk to our players about treating the girls they date with respect and kindness. We remind them they are dating someone else's daughter or sister and treat them how they would want their own family members to be treated. Yes, some players don't have a sister, and so can't relate, but they all have a mother, and we tell them they need to treat that other mother's child with respect.

We discuss the consequences of sexual activity. This could be an unwanted pregnancy, STDs, or just simply using girls for our own pleasure. We want our players to be aware of what they are doing and make the right choices. If engaged in any physical activity with a girl and she says to stop or says, "no," then that is exactly what it means. Young people are often unprepared for sexual activity.

For this reason, we ask our players to be strong and exercise self-control by not placing themselves in these types of situations. Our players should show self-control and avoid situations where physical contact with women is possible. This is especially true when they become frustrated or rejected. Partner and/or domestic abuse is a crime for which the repercussions are immense. Players should remove themselves from any situation in which they feel angry.

Another area we address is racism, homophobia, and discrimination. Our school has students from diverse religious, ethnic, and sexual orientation backgrounds. Regardless of a person's background, we preach love and respect for everyone. We cannot stress the importance of this enough. We want our players to accept and embrace diversity as a positive way to look at others and understand and empathize with them. The only way to do this is to observe, listen, ask questions, and share feelings with others who differ from us. Be aware of the language and tone used. Sometimes, our players do not know that the things they say, post, retweet, or share may be offensive to groups that differ from them. We want our players to embrace diversity and show respect.

Finally, we talk about staying away from unhealthy lifestyles that may affect us beyond our years in high school. There are a variety of vices that can lead young people down a very dark path that may be difficult to overcome in the future. Whether it is abusing drugs, consuming pornography, or partaking in criminal activity, we try to do the best we can to educate our players. We discuss the consequences and effects of engaging in any activity that may lead to a loss of freedom, lifestyle, opportunities, or life. We address these sensitive topics as often as we can but may need extra support from parents and educators.

GIVING BACK

One important area not directly related to our players is the idea of giving back to the coaching community. I know I would not be where I am today had it not been for the coaches who helped me grow throughout the years. I make it a point to share as many ideas and information with as many coaches as I can. Whether it is giving clinic presentations, staff in-services, or one-on-one talks, I want to provide as much knowledge as I can provide. While I don't profess to have all the answers, and I am far from perfect, we have ideas and thoughts that have stood the test of time that others may benefit from. I find tremendous joy in being able to provide others with things that have worked for us. I believe imitation is the greatest form of flattery, and I have no issues with others doing things the way we do them. A major reason I wrote this book is because of the idea of giving back.

SUMMARY OF WINNING THE WRONG WAY

In conclusion, I devoted this chapter to ideas, beliefs, and concepts that go beyond the gridiron. So many of us in the coaching profession have a deep passion for what we do and a desire to help young people become the best version of themselves. Sometimes, in our quest for victories and championships, we lose focus on what truly matters with coaching. Our job is much bigger than wins and losses. We have a tremendous responsibility to educate the young people who we coach. It is for this reason that we must never lose sight of why we are coaching. It is to help build outstanding young people who will be successful years beyond the time we shared with them. I desire for my former players to reach out years later and tell me they became who they are today because of our program. Nothing generates more excitement, happiness, and pure purpose in life than hearing these words.

10

KEEPING A BALANCE: FAITH, FAMILY, FOOTBALL

"The challenge of work life balance is without question one of the most significant struggles faced by modern man."

—Steven Covey, Author

One of the toughest challenges of being a professional, regardless of your chosen career, is keeping a balance between your job and personal life. This is especially true in the coaching profession. One of the biggest reasons I stayed at the high school level was to ensure that I did not have to move my family around the country. While I know plenty of coaches who have done it, either at the high school, college, or professional level, I know the strain it puts on the family to move around. I never wanted my family to go through this. There are several coaches I know whose marriages fell apart. Why?

The job demanded too much time and energy, leaving little for the family. I knew from very early on in my coaching career that I did not want to be another divorce statistic or have kids who never saw their dad. Being a great husband and father was more important than being a brilliant coach. I still strive to be the best coach I can be, but it's not my sole reason for coaching. Coaching does not define me; it is merely something I do. This is the same message I try to preach to our players. How can I teach our players about being excellent husbands and fathers if I don't show it? I want my players to see that you can excel in your profession and be a great family man, even though I am not an expert in either.

The coaching profession is very demanding and requires a lot of our time. Coaches with Type A personalities like things done their way. Our obligations never seem to end. Practice plans, off-season workouts, fundraising, working with various people, game planning, and more. It's a constant barrage of tasks that require competence and efficiency. Without balance and a system, you'll burn out yourself and your family. A plan is crucial for this task.

FAITH AND MENTAL HEALTH

It all starts with you. Self-care and balance can make you an effective family man and coach. For me, a major part of that starts with my faith. Jesus Christ, my Lord and Savior, governs my life as a Christian. My desire to be the best version of myself starts and ends with pleasing God. At the end of my life, I want to stand tall before God and for him to say, "Well done, my faithful servant." In a profession that requires football players to be gruff and tough, being a Christian may not seem to be a natural fit.

Nothing could be further from the truth. Many players and coaches were tough on the field but faithful followers of Christ. It is a misnomer to characterize Christians as weak. The list of Christian football players is extensive. Google search provides many examples of men who are both.

My faith has been the only thing that has kept me sane. Praying when things aren't going well is very comforting. This is true when facing life's challenges. Trusting God provides an unparalleled sense of peace and joy. His Word, which I try to read daily in my bible, gives me purpose and direction for my life. It helps me keep things in perspective and not sweat the small stuff. Prayer and reflection are necessary for me to do this.

One of my daily practices is to wake up early, take out my journal (more of a logbook), and write my daily prayers and a list of things I am grateful for. This reminds me of the good things in my life. This helps me maintain a daily perspective and be grateful for the abundance of good things I have, regardless of what's happening. Afterward, I journal my thoughts and feelings while reading the Bible. This is how I stay connected to God and prioritize what is important to Him and myself. I highly recommend reading Proverbs in the Bible. This book holds 31 chapters, one for each day of the month, and abundant pearls of wisdom. If you read it enough times, eventually, these verses become part of your DNA.

Finally, attending church service weekly has been very beneficial for me. Church is a place where I can go to worship God and hear a message from our pastor that often relates to my struggles. Attending church is not enough; living each day as if in His service is essential. God wants consistency in our behavior every day, not just on Sundays.

Attending church for me is one way that I stay grounded and balanced in my life.

Another practice I do to stay mentally healthy is reading. I am a voracious reader, devouring books every chance I get. The subjects typically have to do with leadership, managing teams, and organizations. I also read about football topics (either team building, developing culture, or scheme ideas). Reading various history subjects (as a person who teaches and loves history, these are the books I read the most) is enjoyable. Occasionally, I will read fiction, but these are far and few between, as there are so many true stories out there that read like fiction. I typically read about a book a month and shoot for 12 books a year. Some years, I have read more since some books are shorter than others, while other years, I may not reach that goal as some books are bigger than others. I try to read as much as I can for several reasons.

First, John Wooden believed our relationships and the books we read shape our lives. I have found both to be very true. We are who we are because of what we fill our minds with. From our opinions and ideas to our thoughts and beliefs, those who we meet and the information we gain shape all of this. Second, I love to learn new things, if for nothing else, it gives me a sense of growing in knowledge. Learning about new things gives me a sense of growth and shapes my thoughts and beliefs based on the information and ideas I gain. I also enjoy gaining new perspectives about topics I have read about in the past. Third, reading offers my mind an escape from all the other things that dominate it daily. It allows me to take a break from the variety of tasks that fill my day up. Finally, reading gives me a sense of peace that few other activities provide.

It's important to focus on other aspects of your life for mental well-being. If all you do is football and/or football-related activities, you will find yourself quickly out of balance.

PHYSICAL HEALTH (EATING AND EXERCISE)

The physical health aspect of coaching is often overlooked, particularly during the season. Our time spent watching films, game planning, practicing, and playing games can cause our physical health to deteriorate. Not getting enough sleep, poor eating habits, and not doing physical activity contribute to this. We neglect our bodies because we feel that we just don't have the time to take care of them. I will be the first to admit that I am guilty of all of this every season, but I have gotten better over the years. The older I get, the better I get by doing some simple practices.

Getting enough sleep during the season has always been a challenge for me. Whether I used that time at night watching films or getting ready for the next day, I have struggled to get enough sleep each year. One thing I have done to address this is to set a time limit on how much I do at night. I will typically give myself an hour to do what I need to do and then stop. While I have not always been good at sticking to the allotted time, I have tried to each night. On Saturday afternoons, once we have completed doing our game planning in the morning, I sneak in a nap as well. This has helped me to catch up on lost sleep throughout the week. Sundays are almost always a rest day. I rarely do anything football-related on Sunday other than watching an NFL game with the family.

Eating healthy is another area that I have focused on maintaining, not only during the season but year-round. I keep a balanced diet to ensure that I am putting excellent fuel into my body. I'm mindful of what I eat each day, from breakfast to lunch. Staying hydrated with lots of water is vital, especially during the summer and early fall when the weather is still hot. I stay away from energy drinks as the side effects are too much for me to handle, but I am guilty of having a cup of coffee each morning. Finally, dinner at night typically involves something relatively healthy across the board. I try not to eat fast food during the season unless necessary. These eating habits have made me feel better throughout the day and given me the energy I need to do what I need to do.

Exercise is another area that has become increasingly more difficult for me each year. I have tried different physical activities throughout the years, but none of them have been consistent. Each year offers a new set of challenges in managing my time, so rather than try to pick one thing to do, I will mix it up and change up what I do. One day, I may walk or jog before leaving for work. Another day, I may do the same at work. Other times, I may do something when I get home at night. The point is, get in some form of exercise. It really doesn't matter what you do, as long as you do something. From staying fit to relieving stress, the benefits of doing exercise far outweigh the prospect of not doing anything.

MAINTAINING A BALANCE WITH YOUR FAMILY

Once you have addressed your own mental and physical health, you must make your family your next priority. The simplest and easiest way to do this is to create ways to share time with them.

When I met with Coach Ladouceur, the former head football coach of De La Salle H. S, I asked him how he maintained a balance between football and his family. He simply said, "Don't bring football home." When I questioned him on this further, he elaborated on the idea. Once he left school, before he walked into the house, he had to clear his mind of everything football-related and focus on being a husband and a father.

Whatever had happened at practice, good or bad, you had to divorce your mind from it and be present with your family. This meant that unless your wife brought football up, you did not talk about it or allow your mind to wander to football-related thoughts. I found this concept ridiculously profound and yet simple. The challenge, of course, was being able to do what he suggested.

In my early years, I found it extremely difficult to execute this practice. I often wanted to talk about my frustrations, but my family didn't understand. They did not know what I was talking about. They only knew that I was feeling agitated and irritable. This, of course, did not go over well with my wife. I had to learn how to compartmentalize my feelings about what was going on at work and simply be happy to be home with them. The more troublesome part was not allowing my mind to wander and think about football stuff while at home. This took a lot of practice on my part and patience on my wife's. Eventually, I was able to accomplish this, and the longer I coached, the more my wife and family appreciated it.

Involve your wife and children in football activities. For your wife, it could be something as simple as attending a practice or two during the week. She could walk the track around the field while the team is practicing or be more involved, like helping with the team meals. As for your kids, depending on their age, you could have them attend practices and help with water or be a ball boy on game day. Fundraising events or social gatherings are a great way to include your family as well. One practice we have done over the years is to invite a group of players over to our home in the off-season for a meal and team bonding. Again, this is another way to include your family. Regardless of the event or activity, try to be creative by including your family in your football activities. This will go a long way in making them feel they are a part of what you do.

Another practice that I found very helpful is making date nights with my wife during the season (out-of-season is given). This gives you and your wife the chance to get away from the kids and work on your relationship. We typically go out to dinner on Saturday evenings, which allows us a break from cooking and gives us alone time to talk about whatever we want. By doing this, you are showing your wife that even during your busiest time of the year, you are attempting to keep her a priority. This has been highly beneficial to us, especially with the difficulties of being a married couple, with one of us being a coach. I make it a point to buy flowers or cards during the season. Again, this shows her I am making her a priority even as I am doing what I am passionate about. Finally, by doing these things, I am showing my kids that our marriage is my priority, as well as showing them how a husband and wife are supposed to act. While not perfect, we model the behaviors that we feel will benefit our children in their future relationships.

Stay connected with your kids and their activities. When they were younger, this simply meant I played games with them, wrestled with them, or read books to them. It doesn't have to be anything elaborate. Just making the time, quality time, to focus on them is more than enough to show your kids that they are your priority. When my kids got older and began taking part in youth sports, I made it a priority to not only attend their events but, if time permitted, help coach the teams they were on. Coaching your kids is a topic I will speak on in a later chapter, but for this chapter, I will simply say that just being a part of your kids' team and being present is vital. Make attending your kids' games or the events they take part in your priority.

OTHER ACTIVITIES AND THEIR EFFECTS

It's appropriate to offer a word of caution to those coaches who take part in activities that do not involve your family or take you away from them. I have never been a big golfer, bowler, or dart thrower, let alone a hunter, fisherman, or any kind of artisan. So maybe it was easier for me, but I know that doing any of these activities might take you away from your family, which may cause problems. I am not saying that if you do any of these activities, you're a bad person. Some might even say that doing these or other activities is how you maintain your sanity. This may be true. It needs to be done in moderation while keeping a balance of sharing time with your family. In my mind, coaching football takes so much of my time and energy that I could not justify anything that would take time away from my wife and kids. Again, I am not saying anyone who does this is a bad person. But with such little time we have left over after coaching, consider either significantly cutting back on them or pressing pause on doing them.

Make sure your family is ok with you doing them or with you being gone. Only prioritize this if you want to stay connected and married to your family! Let's be serious: if we want family happiness, we need to reconsider our activities outside of coaching.

SUMMARY OF KEEPING A BALANCE

Whatever you do, you need to make some decisions about what your priorities are going to be. For me, it always came down to my faith, my family, and then coaching football. While your priorities may be different, whatever you decide to do, keep a balance in your life in order to be the best version of yourself.

11

COACHING YOUR OWN CHILDREN: NOTHING BETTER, NOTHING MORE CHALLENGING

"A lot of times, the expectations of you are so high that no matter what you do, you will never live up to those expectations. So, you better go out and do the best you can and enjoy it."

—JOHN ELWAY

On our very first date, my wife and I discussed the topics of marriage, raising a family, and how we would share our life. This, of course, is highly unusual for a first date. We were both close to 30 and knew what we wanted in a relationship, so why continue if we didn't agree? It was during this date that we both expressed a desire to have three children, and in a perfect world, we would have two boys and a girl, in that order. This was beyond our control, but it was fun to talk about. As we got married in 1999, we were fortunate enough to have two sons and a daughter, in that order, just as we had discussed.

When our oldest son could take part in sports, we signed him up for t-ball. This began my journey of coaching my children throughout their elementary, junior high, and high school careers. I had always had a desire to be a part of my children's sports experience for a variety of reasons. One, it was a way that we could share time and bond as parents and children. Second, my chosen profession of being a coach gave me some insight into how to be a positive role model for both other children and my own.

Finally, I wanted to ensure that whoever was the coach of my children's team was someone who understood the value and purpose of youth sports. I had witnessed coaches destroying kids' sports experiences with their behavior and misguided coaching. I wanted my kids' sports experience to be positive. Not that I felt I had the market cornered on how to be a positive coach and influence kids, but I had enough experience in coaching that I could contribute positively.

PARENT-CHILD RELATIONSHIP

The first thing you need to do when you decide to coach your own children is to ensure you are doing it for the right reasons. This can be very difficult to define and understand, as everyone has their own opinion on what exactly the right reasons are. For me, it begins with protecting the parent-child relationship.

Separate yourself from being a parent when you are on the field or court of play when coaching your own children. This means you have to treat your child the same as the other children and avoid "daddy ball." This is the idea of making your child the center of your team, for which all other children are simply there to support and help your child excel. Parents sometimes coach their child's team to make them the star. Nothing good comes from doing this. Showing favoritism creates an unhealthy situation for your child and hurts the other team members. There may be times when your child is, in fact, the most talented player on the team. When this is the case, you need to work extra hard to ensure the other members of the team are contributing meaningfully and feel like they are just as important.

Along those same lines, you must ensure you are not being harder on your own child compared to the other participants. Remember that your child is simply another member of the team who deserves to be treated fairly, just like everyone else. Both are essential to ensure that your child's participation in sports is healthy for both of you.

Once you leave the field or court of play, you need to take your coaching hat off and put your parents' hat on. This can be very challenging for many, as it is in our nature to "help" our child once practice is over. As hard as it may be, you need to fight the urge to give your child unsolicited advice. Just be your child's parent and love them unconditionally. Should your child ask you for advice or suggestions on what they can do to improve, focus your advice on their effort and any basic skills that they may improve on? Avoid the temptation of using this as a gateway to giving them everything that's in your head on what you think they need to do to be better. Keep it short and simple. Should your child continue to ask questions, then provide the answers. Be sure not to offer to do drills with them in the backyard or the park unless they ask you. Again, if they do, then do what you can to help them while also keeping it simple and fun.

Doing these things are just some things you can do to protect the parent-child relationship.

MAKE IT FUN

We are all competitive and want to win, but this should be secondary to the idea of making both practice and games fun. Yes, winning is fun, but you spend a lot more time in practice than you do in games, so this is where you must work hard to make the game entertaining for the players. This is especially true when your own child is on the team. Remember, your child should play because they want to play and, in most cases, with their friends. If you're going to be a coach on your child's team, either as an assistant coach or the head coach, make it a priority to include activities that make it fun. Make drills competitive, add competitions, and use schoolyard games for conditioning. Ensure the kids have fun. Your child needs to see you actively doing the sport they are doing for fun.

IT'S YOUR CHILD'S EXPERIENCE, NOT YOURS

One of the biggest challenges I faced when my two boys were growing up was ensuring that they did not feel obligated or expected to play football. As children of a football coach, they were constantly around the program. Whether it was at practices or games, they were always around watching me coach. Or, in most cases, playing their own games with the balls or bags on the sideline or end zone. If they ever played football, I wanted them to make that decision on their own. One way I tried to ensure this was by encouraging them to play as many sports as possible to see what they liked and didn't like. Whether it was baseball, rugby, basketball, swimming, or any other sport, I allowed them to take part and, when possible, assisted the teams that they were a part of. In most cases, I was the assistant coach, helping the team in whatever capacity the head coach wanted. In doing this, I was simply a part of their experience and avoided many of the challenges that arise with being a head coach with a child on the team.

When my oldest was seven years old, he asked if he could play football. When his mother and I tried to convince him to try out flag football, we were met with a stern and determined child who did not want any of it. He wanted to play tackle football, just like the players in our program were playing. We went round and round on the subject, not sure if we wanted to let him play tackle football at such a young age. We consulted people we knew who had experience allowing their young children to play tackle football. The advice we received was very helpful. Most of them stated that if that is what their children wanted to do, then they allowed it. I made the final decision to allow him to play when I felt confident that it was what he wanted to do for himself and not because I was a football coach. The same was true for my second son when he came of age to play as well. Regardless of any difficulties, I ensured they finished their youth football seasons. Once the season was over, we would then either take a break from playing a sport or move on to the next sport they were interested in. In each case, I made sure that they articulated to me that the reason they wanted to play football (or any other sport) was because it was what they wanted to do. I didn't want my kids to do anything out of obligation.

For us, this was critical. Over the years of coaching high school football, time and time again, I have seen so many young men play football out of a sense of duty for their parents or family. It is very easy to spot as often the kids are miserable and are clearly not enjoying the sport. They are the ones who simply show up, do the bare minimum at practice, and bolt after practice is over. They are simply there to please their parents.

On the other side of this, I have seen many parents who live their lives vicariously through their kids. This usually involves having both unrealistic expectations of their child's abilities and a passion for the game. This, too, is very easy to spot. It's the parents who are constantly screaming at their children while they are playing, pleading with them to play better than what they are displaying. They are also the ones who are yelling at the coaches, the officials, or the opposing teams' players, all to promote their child's ability or performance. In either case, when a child is playing for their parents and/or the parents are living vicariously through their kids, it is never a beneficial situation. With us, I wanted to do everything possible to ensure my kids wanted to play sports for themselves and not to please us.

COACH, BUT DON'T COACH

If I were going to assist on any of my children's youth sports teams as an assistant coach, one strategy I would employ was to coach without coaching my child. I usually worked out an arrangement with another coach to coach each other's child. This allowed us to be a part of our child's youth sports experience without having to coach our own kid directly. Sure, sometimes I would go to my child's coach and offer advice or suggestions on what my child needed to improve upon. But I always felt it was better received coming from some other coach rather than me. It didn't matter if I knew exactly what needed to be done for my child to be successful. If it came from me, my kids would often have a hard time differentiating between parent and coach. It almost always seemed to be much better received when it was coming from another coach. This was especially true in youth sports. Did this change a little once they began playing high school football? Yes, but I still tried as much as possible to have another coach provide the instruction for my kids. I found this strategy very helpful in maintaining a much healthier relationship with my own children.

TRANSITION FROM YOUTH SPORTS TO HIGH SCHOOL SPORTS

Being a part of my children's youth sports experience was a walk in the park compared to when they entered high school. For whatever reason, things seemed to get more challenging once my kids were on the same campus where I worked. I guess that the biggest reason for these challenges was the fact that they were no longer little kids but were now teenagers. I remember all those parents who used to say to me, "Enjoy them now while they are young because once they become teenagers, it's a whole new game," and thought, not my kids. Things will always be blissful and easy. Boy, was I wrong! I'm not saying my kids were monsters, but there were plenty of challenges that came up once they were in high school and taking part in sports.

One of the biggest challenges is the fact that they are now where you work. They must learn to cope with the new situation of being a teacher/coach's kid while also being distinct from the other students. It's almost as if other students and teachers expect your kids to be better than everyone else in all phases. This is not absolute, but it sure felt like there was additional pressure on both the kids and me to differ from the general student population. Whether this was reality or self-imposed paranoia, I still felt it, and I know my kids did, too. There are some things that we all needed to work out as we progressed through four years of high school.

From an academic standpoint, I helped all my kids with their course selection and teachers. One of the few perks that an on-campus teacher gets is helping their own children who attend the school navigate their class schedules. I wanted my kids to take rigorous courses but balance them with the activities they would be doing. This took some effort, but we got it all worked out.

As far as playing sports, all the previously mentioned ideas and concepts that were used for youth sports applied to high school. While they were on the teams I coached, I ensured I was challenging but fair with them. I sought advice from my assistant coaches to avoid any favoritism. While I was not perfect at this, I felt like I did a decent job of allowing my kids' own abilities and talents to determine their playing time and roles while on the team. Both of my boys played freshman football, where they both were contributors to their team's success. Following their freshman year, they both played varsity from their sophomore year through their senior year. Both of them played significantly and contributed to the team's overall success. While this part was rewarding as a dad, it was even more rewarding knowing that both of them earned every second of their playing time, which had nothing to do with me.

DEALING WITH INJURIES

Navigating injuries my children had from playing football was the most troublesome part of coaching them. Both of them suffered significant trauma from playing, and the toll it took on them, both physically and mentally, was something that I had not expected.

When my oldest son was a freshman, he sustained a fractured shoulder blade when he was hit from behind in his last game. While the injury was painful and ended his season, he healed fine and could continue his playing career. It was during his sophomore year that things got really serious.

As a linebacker, he was usually involved in violent collisions, which are commonplace for the position. While observing him in practice following our third game, I saw him make a routine tackle in practice. We rarely took guys to the ground but simply would hit and wrap up opposing ball carriers. I noticed he stumbled, lost his balance, and shook his head. I immediately called him out of the drill and had him see our athletic trainer.

When there was a break, I went over to him and the trainer to find out what was happening. He revealed to both the trainer and me that he felt dizzy, nauseous, and had blurred vision, all signs that he had sustained a concussion. We discovered he had hurt his head the week before but had told no one. He was afraid of being taken off the field.

To say I was furious was an understatement. I made it clear to all team players to report head injuries to the staff. I realized in two weeks that my son had sustained what we suspected was his first and second concussion. Over the next four weeks, my son would miss 20 days of school as he tried to recover from the effects of his concussions. It was frightening for us to witness him go through light sensitivity, dizziness, and difficulty in focusing and thinking. Eventually, his symptoms would dissipate, and he would regain feeling like himself again. We struggled with deciding to let him continue to play at all that season. Eventually, we allowed him to play. He returned for the last two games of the season, only to break his forearm on the last series of our playoff game.

Those two years of injuries were enough for his mother and me to consider ending his career for him. We were genuinely concerned about his physical well-being beyond playing football. He, of course, was not having any of this. He insisted that football was the only thing that kept him motivated and connected in school, despite our attempts to break this connection. Fortunately, he would play both his Junior and senior years with minimal injuries, apart from the occasional sprained ankle. I sometimes question whether we made the right decision to allow him to continue. But playing football was something that he thoroughly enjoyed and wanted to do. He would complete his high school playing experience and decided not to pursue football in college. This was an enormous relief for both of his parents.

My son's concussion gave me a new appreciation for athletes with head injuries. Concussions are one of those injuries that you don't see and can never fully tell how serious it is or how long the recovery is going to last. While players of mine in the past had sustained concussions, it was always something that I struggled with to know when they would come back. I admit I doubted some players' concussions were genuine.

After seeing what my son went through, I have gained a whole new perspective on the injury and recovery time to come back. Never again will I ever question a player who says they injured their head or when they can return to play. I will leave that to medical professionals, parents, and the player himself to let me know if they are okay with returning to play.

We were worried about our second son's health when he played football. In his freshman year, he played relatively injury-free. He amassed a ton of yards and touchdowns as a running back and was ready to be our starter on the varsity level in his sophomore year. He played well in his second year until he got injured with no contact in the seventh game. It confirmed his and my worst fears when the doctor on the sideline stated he believed he had torn his ACL. A visit to the doctor and MRI the following week confirmed the diagnosis. It was devastating to all of us, mostly him. He could not understand that making a routine cut on field that he had done so effortlessly and routinely resulted in a catastrophic injury. For me, it was crushing on so many levels. We had lost our starting RB, who was on pace to gain a lot of yards and touchdowns. It was heartbreaking to see my son lose his spot, which he had worked hard for, because of something he couldn't control. He had surgery, therapy, and a second surgery over the next nine months. While not 100% healed from the surgery, he gave it a valiant effort to play and compete that next season. He would miss a few games as other parts of his body failed him because of the recovery process.

Following the season, he committed himself to getting ready for his senior season, which would have been in the fall of 2020. Then COVID hit in March of that year, postponing all the players' seasons that fall until the spring of 2021. Two weeks before they cleared us to play a shortened season that none of us was sure was going to happen, he tore his MCL while snowboarding. He attempted to play on it four weeks later in our first game, only to re-injure it when he got tackled, thus ending his high school career. I was heartbroken for him on so many levels. For reasons I will discuss in a later chapter, he had gone through arguably the toughest three years of high school any kid could have gone through. But through it all, he never quit, kept a positive attitude, and never let what life had dealt him bring him down.

The mental strain and emotional roller coaster that both my son's injuries played on my mind was unimaginable. To see both of them endure what they did and still maintain some sense of sanity is truly remarkable. I could not be prouder to see both come out of their experience the way they did. I like to think that because of their challenges, they will be stronger and more resilient young men because of it. For me, it has taken a lot of prayer, soul searching, and reevaluating as both a coach and parent to continue coaching. Despite the injuries, my sons were thankful for the chance to play football with me as their coach. That was enough for me to continue coaching.

SUMMARY OF COACHING YOUR CHILDREN

Being a part of your children's athletic experience can be a very rewarding and enjoyable experience. You must have the right motives, mindset, and attitude. It cannot be stressed enough that you must have a very honest reason to coach your own children. It should be for all the reasons stated above, but more than anything else, it should be about sharing time with your kids and watching them grow as young people. I believe with all my heart that I coached my children for the right reasons and provided a positive, not perfect, experience for them and me.

12

DEALING WITH 21ST CENTURY CULTURE: ISSUES OF TODAY

"Just like moons and like suns, With the certainty of tides, Just like hopes springing high, Still I'll rise."

—MAYA ANGELOU

Man, have times changed. The '70s and '80s seemed simpler. Kids have to deal with mind-boggling challenges and obstacles today. I no longer see similarities in the experiences of kids today and ours. The world is reaching extra levels of insanity. I now give more attention to topics important for our players' growth than I did when I first started coaching. Before, I focused on football strategy, skills, and drills. Today, I spend more time discussing life with our players. I do the best I can to educate, guide, and inspire them to overcome what I perceive to be the ever-changing climate our world has become.

SOCIAL MEDIA

When I was in middle and high school, cell phones and computers were in their infancy. I still remember my first computer class in my junior year of high school, banging away on the keys of our Commodore 64k's, thinking these things were a fad and would pass. Boy, was I wrong. From Atari to Colecco to the first Apple II, technology has advanced beyond our imagination and ability to keep up. The internet's progress caused things to grow and expand. I got my first cell phone and computer in the early 90s. I never imagined we'd have smartphones with such capabilities. While this technology has helped bring our world a lot closer together and has provided us with a wealth of information, it has not been without its problems. Dr. Jean M. Twenge details in her book, *iGen*, how technology has created a generation of young people who are having difficulty in life. To ensure students become what we hope, we must help them with technology.

In 2008, when the first iPhone came out with its touch and swipe screens, little did we know we would have a computer at our fingertips. These devices promise to revolutionize our lives in a variety of ways. It has done that with some very concerning consequences.

First, you have the challenge of monitoring the content young people can access. Pornography, drug culture, and dangerous activities are all available with the swipe of a finger. It doesn't equip young people to handle adult internet material. They expose children to inappropriate content that steals much of their innocence while growing up.

Second, content on their devices is affecting how young people think, dress, and act. Young minds' impressionability is the target content providers aim to capitalize on. The content produced by these providers lacks regulation and oversight. Young people have trouble discerning the truth from this false sense of reality. The internet does not guarantee accuracy or authenticity, yet some young people accept its content as truth. This can sway youth because of the challenge of distinguishing truth from falsehood. Teaching our children how to fact-check and determine what is true and what is fake is necessary.

Third, app makers and providers have saturated young people's brains with a never-ending barrage of content that does not allow for breaks. Teens (and adults) can't seem to stop scrolling through content on social media. This constant intake of mind-numbing content cheats our young people in real-life relationships. They spend hours digesting information with little to no interaction with real human beings. Being on their phone causes young people to miss out on life going on around them. Every spare second a teenager is not engaged in an activity, you will see them on their phone.

Students often sit with other groups, walk to class, or wait at their desks, all while using their phones. People are constantly using their phones in the community - at stoplights, in lines, and while waiting. Encourage young people to put down their phones and pay attention to their surroundings. By doing this, we may cut down on their screen time.

Our children are unaware of the consequences of their actions online. This includes what they are posting/re-posting, "liking," or clicking "favorite" when on the internet using their phones. Young people are unaware of the consequences of what they post online, from inappropriate videos and pictures to their likes. Business owners, professionals, and college football recruiters have told me they check the content that young people put out there. This can cause missed opportunities because of social media content.

Argue for free speech all you want, but people are going to judge you, fairly or unfairly, based on your digital appearance and footprint. We must teach this to our young people and explain this to them.

Young people now measure their self-worth by their views, likes, and followers. Young people feel anxious, lonely, and depressed because of the pressure to 'keep up.' Many young people today feel left out because of a false sense of exclusion. Allowing my kids to have smartphones in Junior High has led to parental regret. I convinced myself that they needed to have one so that I could stay in touch with them and connect with them easier. This was a huge mistake. My kids will tell you it is the one thing I regret more than anything as it pertains to raising them. I would delay giving my kids smartphones if I could do it again. We need to educate ourselves and our children about when to give them a device and how to use it responsibly.

We have taken some steps to cut down on our players' phone time by taking some very simple, practical steps. Anytime we get together, we require the players to put their phones on silent mode on the floor underneath where they are sitting. This way, the constant notifications do not distract them. I prohibit phones in the weight room or on the field. Addressing what they post, like retweeting, etc., is another area we have discussed with them. We make sure they understand the importance of not embarrassing themselves, their family, our school, or our football program.

MENTAL HEALTH

Students experience anxiety, depression, and a host of other mental health challenges. Regardless of the causes, young people today are experiencing all kinds of mental health issues that need to be addressed. I'm still learning about all these conditions, but I'm more aware and sensitive to young people's feelings. The days of saying "toughen up" and "get over it" are gone. Young people need to be taught how to persevere through their struggles.

I urge players and students to talk about their thoughts. Expressing your thoughts and feelings as opposed to repressing them is the healthiest way I know of to start the healing and recovery process. While I am not a trained mental health professional, my experience has shown me that being available is a tremendous help. Listening to people's problems can make them feel better about themselves and their situation.

Being heard and understood can provide comfort. If a player expresses something that I feel I am not qualified to handle, I will refer them to someone who can.

Awareness goes a long way. Having positive mental health has become something that everyone should strive for. Celebrities, athletes, and business professionals have discussed their mental challenges, which gives us hope. It has allowed anyone who is struggling not to feel isolated and like they are the only ones dealing with internal struggles. This helps raise awareness of the importance of positive mental health.

SUICIDE

According to the CDC, teenage suicide is the #2 leading cause of death after accidental death in America. I find this both sad and disturbing. We can affect young people in this area.

The importance of mental health has reached additional levels of awareness and acceptance in our nation. No longer are we telling people to "toughen up" and ignore obvious signs of mental anguish. It is becoming more acceptable for young people to open up about their inner struggles. Our students have experienced positive effects on their well-being as they discuss their inner thoughts. We encourage them to inform us of their anxiety and stress, which often eases their feelings. Sometimes, what is being communicated to us is more than we can address, and we direct our players to a wealth of resources available to them. We provide players with help and support from school counselors, healthcare providers, and parents.

Diligence on our part as coaches must be of paramount importance. Knowing our players is important to identifying potential issues. Daily intimacy building with our players is necessary to achieve this. This comes with time, patience, and commitment on our part to know our players. We strive to be familiar with our players so we can assist them when needed.

SITUATIONAL AWARENESS

In a later chapter, I will share the events that transpired on our campus involving an active shooter. But for this discussion, I will focus on having situational awareness. Some people use violence to harm others for social, political, religious, or suicidal reasons. Regardless of their reason, some people choose a gun to carry out their plan to the extreme detriment of other human beings. We must do what we can to help our young people learn strategies that may save lives.

One thing we do with our players is have discussions about having situational awareness, regardless of where they are. This includes both on campus and in the community. The first thing we talk about is understanding your surroundings. This involves watching people and getting a feel for the mood, attitude, and activity that others around them are doing. I'm not suggesting our players be paranoid. But have some situational awareness of others. If something seems out of place, remove yourself or notify someone in authority. They should go on as usual, but at least they attempted to protect themselves and others.

Second, we tell our players to have an escape strategy. Always know where the escape routes are, regardless of your location. It's important they know both indoor and outdoor exits. It may seem paranoid, but it's reality. I would rather have our players vigilant of their surroundings than for something to happen to them because they were oblivious.

DRUGS AND ALCOHOL USE

Drug and alcohol use is a major problem in our society, but it is especially prevalent in younger individuals. Young people are entering rehab at younger ages than before.

Drugs and alcohol have affected young people, such as increased accessibility and acceptance in movies, TV shows, and music. It is important to talk honestly with young people about the risks of drug abuse. While marijuana has become legal in many states across our nation, it does not change the fact that many young people are abusing it. I often inform our players that a good deal of methamphetamine, heroin, opioid, or other illegal drug addicts did not start that way. They moved from marijuana to more powerful drugs in search of a longer high. From my experience, this is often true, but not always.

Despite being widely accepted, alcohol is a constant danger that young people need reminders of.

Whether it is alcohol or drugs, we are talking to our players about the negative effects consuming these will have on them. Using these will not help them reach their goals on the field. We often make poor decisions while under the influence, leading to negative consequences. Driving under the influence is one example. Getting into fights is another. Getting into a sexual situation where an assault may happen is another. We stress to our players that there is nothing good that comes out of using drugs or alcohol.

Talking about drugs and alcohol is the most effective. I remind them not to go out drinking or using drugs, especially on Friday nights after our games. We discourage players from this activity, although they may think it's fun.

RACIAL, LGBTQIA+, AND POLITICAL ISSUES

Mirroring what is going on in our society, racial, LGBTQIA+, and political issues have filtered down into our students' lives more than I can ever remember. The effects on young people have grown, and we must address them with tolerant and respectful language.

The death of George Floyd sparked protests and made systemic racism a major part of our players' conversations. Racism has been a long-standing problem in all areas of our nation, but tolerance for it has decreased. Terminology and comments that were once okay are no longer permitted. We stress the importance of being sensitive towards all people, regardless of their race or ethnicity. We explain to players why their words may be offensive. Our players no longer use words with disregard for their racial implications.

This also applies to the LGBTQIA+ community. Again, education is the key to the words players use. Using "gay" as a derogatory term is no longer acceptable today. This, as well as other language, may offend someone in the LGBTQIA+ community. We must teach our players what is and is not acceptable. We must teach players to show respect when speaking to people.

There has been a large divide between differing political beliefs in our nation. People reject ideas and opinions that don't align with their beliefs. I've never experienced this level of division before. People reject differing ideas from their own. This breeds negativity and intolerance that is hard to overcome. We don't discuss politics but emphasize respect for other perspectives. This is vital to understanding others and where they are coming from. Young people may find this very challenging. There are so many competing influences in their lives (parents, family, friends, media, etc.) that we must contend with.

SUMMARY OF DEALING WITH 21ST CENTURY CULTURE

If you are going to be a successful coach in the 21st century, the days of coaching Xs and Os without addressing these and other important issues are long gone. We have grown beyond being just a coach. Our role is to coach, mentor, counsel, and advise young people. Those who don't expect this usually don't last very long in coaching, based on my experience. To make a lasting positive impact on players, we must address these topics and others head-on.

13

TRAGEDY AND TRIUMPH: SCHOOL SHOOTING, COVID-19, AND LEAGUE CHAMPS

"Black care rarely sits behind a rider whose pace is fast enough."

—Theodore Roosevelt

The 2018 football season was an emotional roller coaster ride for our family. The season was unique for us in that both our sons were playing on the Varsity football team. My eldest was a senior starting linebacker, and my middle son was a sophomore starting running back. Both were having solid seasons, one on each side of the ball, helping our team to a winning record by the time we reached the seventh game of the season. While running the ball, our middle son went down suddenly without being touched. The medical team on the sideline diagnosed him with a major knee injury (later confirmed to be a torn ACL the following week). They announced he would not return to the game. It altered our game plan, and we ended up losing a very close game. While the loss of him was devastating to him, me, and our team, we kept it together and competed for the rest of the season. We advanced to the first round of the playoffs, beating a team that had defeated us in the previous season's first round. We would lose our quarter-final game, ending our season and my eldest son's high school playing career. Although the 2018 season didn't go as planned, we were thankful for the memories made.

We were excited for the off-season and the start of the 2019 season. My middle son, following successful surgery to repair his torn ACL, was on the road to recovery and was slogging himself back into playing shape. We felt that our off-season weight room program was developing our players into a pretty good team that we felt would be competitive. Then, on the last day of spring practice, our projected starting senior quarterback tore his ACL. This event led to two and a half years of unimaginable events.

THE 2019 SEASON

Once our senior quarterback could not play for the fall, we quickly elevated our junior quarterback to the starting position. We worked all summer to prepare him for the game while also improving other aspects of our team. He brought a unique skill set, which altered what we were planning on doing offensively. We got him ready to compete once the season started. As we began playing games, our team struggled to find an identity. Some players focused too much on their off-field activities, resulting in poor team performance. The harder we tried to rein them in, the tougher it became to get any team chemistry going. Each week saw us make multiple mistakes that cost us victories in games. My son was still trying to work himself back into the lineup. He dealt with nagging injuries to other parts of his body that were caused by his compensating for his recovering knee. Poor air quality caused by nearby brush fires forced us to reschedule two games from Friday to Saturday. This change of routine was not good for an already fragile group of players. By the time we reached our last game, we had gone winless in the league for the first time since 2003. We eked out a victory for our last game to finish 5th in the league, but our record ensured that we were out of the playoffs.

The end of the season left me feeling emotionally drained and discouraged. I interviewed returning players after our loss and found out they were upset by the outgoing players' lack of commitment. They created an expectation list and consequences for failing to comply for their senior year. Their determination encouraged me, and I felt reinvigorated for the 2020 season.

NOVEMBER 14, 2019

The morning of Thursday, November 14, 2019, started like most days. It had been a week and a half since our season was over. I was finishing up our player post-season interviews in my office, which was next to my classroom in the same building. Many of the football players were in my first-period class, either doing homework or socializing. I had just finished interviewing one underclassman. When I came into my classroom to call in one of the last players I needed to interview, one player said, "Coach, I think there is an active shooter on campus!" I asked him if he was joking (the player in question had a sense of humor, albeit this was not his normal type of joke), to which he responded, "No, I'm serious!" I asked him a second time for confirmation if he was joking. He said, "No!" again, explaining that his brother texted him about students scrambling off campus in a panic. Once he said this, I went into what I call "cyborg mode." Maybe it was my Marine training or the active shooter drills we had rehearsed on our campus. It could have been the many movies I had seen. Or maybe it was the fact that both my middle son and daughter (she had begun her freshman year on campus that fall) were in my classroom with me. Fear and calmness took over as my mind went on autopilot.

    I instructed the players to leave their belongings and head to the core space of the building. Upon seeing running for cover outside, I instructed them to enter my room, locked the doors, and turned off the lights. I locked the doors and turned off the lights in the two empty adjacent classrooms by going through the core of our building. The remaining classroom of our building, which had students in it, was in lockdown mode. The teacher and students were under their desks, and the lights were off. I returned to the core, where there were 32 students, most of them football players, including my kids. I informed them of our plans. We would remain here quietly, and if anyone attempted to break into the building, we would remain calm and quiet. If any of the doors in the building were breached, I instructed them on what we would do next. We would run up the outside our building that led to the surface street that ran parallel to the campus. We planned to climb over the gate if it was locked and head towards the surrounding neighborhood for safety. I explained everything. I asked them all to grab hands and we prayed. We prayed for everyone's safety, including those still on campus. I ensured all students remained quiet in the core

Tragedy and Triumph: School Shooting, COVID-19, and League Champs

while I repeatedly checked the windows of the four classrooms. To say I was hyper-vigilant was an understatement. The safety of my students was my utmost concern.

As time passed, we used students' phones to access internet messages and reports to understand the situation. While everything was going on, I saw my phone and noticed 20 texts. I quickly scrolled through them and found that my wife had texted me. I simply respond to her, "Kids are with me, we are OK, I love you. Pray for everyone." Several of the messages were from other coaches, family members, friends, and several former players who were police officers. One of them called and told me to wait as help was being dispatched. I called the dad of one of the players in the core with me, who was a sheriff's deputy, for updates. He instructed me to wait for law enforcement to evacuate us, as the situation was still uncertain. He reassured me they flooded the campus with law enforcement officers and that he knew we would be ok.

Living in our community has the advantage of having many civil servants as residents. Teachers, firefighters, and law enforcement officers near our campus were ready to help. We spent two hours in the building core when the player's deputy dad called to inform me of a team of officers in route to our building. Fifteen to twenty officers, some in uniform and others in civilian clothes with tactical gear came to our building and escorted us to the gym. As we walked to the gym, I recall seeing students' belongings scattered all over the place dropped as they fled the campus. Backpacks, books, hats, and even shoes were everywhere. It became abundantly clear to me that this was a major event. That day, I witnessed an unprecedented gathering of law enforcement officers from multiple agencies. Our campus had a lot of police presence, from L.A. County Sheriff to LAPD, Burbank PD, Glendale PD, San Fernando PD, U.S. Marshals, and the FBI. They took us to a church parking lot located next to the campus. School buses then picked us up and drove us to a park where parents could pick their kids up. The media was all over the place, interviewing students and teachers alike. Firefighters, ambulances, and news helicopters were everywhere. Adults and young people were hugging and crying. It was straight out of a movie. The whole thing was surreal.

I remember the events of Columbine H.S. in 1999 like they were yesterday. That event has lingered in my mind for years. I've warned my students over the years about the risk of a school shooting in our community by referencing that tragic event. Maybe it's the social demographic makeup of our community. For reasons unknown to me, I just felt like our community was a place where something horrible like this could happen.

The following days would unveil the truth about that morning. A junior student who was both an athlete and an honor student entered the quad before classes were to begin. He reached into his backpack and pulled out a semi-automatic pistol (it was later determined to be a mail-order ghost gun he had purchased and built). He then fired off several rounds before he turned the gun on himself. In eight seconds, he shot and killed two students, wounded three others, and killed himself. This event forever changed the lives of everyone connected to our school that day.

The rest of the semester up to Christmas break was a blur. We took a week or two off before bringing students back to campus, focusing on making them feel safe. We had grief counselors, therapy dogs, blankets, and all kinds of altered activities. All of which was designed to make our students comfortable being back on campus. In the shooting's aftermath, we froze the students' grades and allowed only room for improvement. This made it easier for everyone. Later that week, the local park held a vigil with 20,000 attendees. The level of community support we received was incredible. It didn't matter if it was someone from our own school or one of our league rivals; everyone was sharing our pain and contributing to the healing process. The phrase "Saugus Strong" came alive and represented our school and communities' desire to overcome the tragedy of that day. I even attended one of our league football teams' playoff games, where they did a moment of silence. They released balloons and chanted "Saugus Strong " five times, then applauded. It was a very touching sign of love shown by the crowd.

I contacted as many football players as possible to offer support. Being in my room comforted many during the shooting. They feared the uncertainty of the events that morning. However, being with me, they felt safe. I had quite a few parents express the same to me either by email, phone call, or in person. Their shared sentiment made me feel good.

We returned to campus in January, still processing the events of November 14, but ready to prepare for the 2020 season. Players prepared to return to normalcy throughout January and February. However, unexpectedly, our world was about to change drastically.

MARCH 16, 2020

I can vividly remember thinking each year I coached what could happen that would cancel an entire football season. Even as a history teacher, I can't ever remember a high school football season ever being canceled. I know it has canceled games for various reasons, but never a season. A war on American soil, as depicted in the movie *Red Dawn* (the original version), was the only possibility I could imagine. Then COVID-19 came and changed everything.

In the early months of 2020, news outlets shared about a virus that was sweeping across Asia and Europe. It reminded me of Bird Flu,

SARS, Swine Flu, and H1N1, illnesses that had come and gone in my lifetime. I assumed that COVID-19 would be the same. Then, things changed in late February and early March. Word that the virus had reached the U.S. and was spreading rapidly became the top news story. With each passing day, the seriousness of the virus was becoming clear. The district warned schools to prepare for virtual instruction starting March 9. None of us knew what exactly that meant as we moved forward that week. However, we were told that if we had not already created Google Classroom pages for our classes, we needed to do so ASAP. They informed us that Friday, March 13, 2020, would be our last day of in-class instruction. We were all in shock at what was happening, but reality set in when, on Monday, March 16, we began what would become our new reality.

This change isolated the students from their friends and activities after transitioning to online learning. We hoped this would be temporary and we'd return to school in April.

The idea of returning to campus and sports was becoming more remote each month. They officially canceled spring sports. Graduation ceremonies for the class of 2020 would be a drive-through event. They canceled all summer sports camps. We were still hoping that our fall season would happen, but with each passing week, even that hope disappeared. It became abundantly clear that our season was in serious jeopardy of ever happening. A year of hope after a school shooting was slipping away.

Once we went to online learning in March, we began conducting Zoom meetings with our football players. We kept connected and prepared our players for the season ahead. The chance of having a season, either full or abbreviated, vanished as weeks passed by in the spring and summer. We hoped for a season in late fall/early winter. We were allowed to meet in person with our players, but the workouts wouldn't be like normal.

They were placed in pods of ten players, with a coach assigned to each one to conduct contact tracing should anyone test positive for COVID-19. They prohibited the indoor use of the weight room or classrooms for meetings. Terms like social distancing and wearing masks while running around on the field became the new norm. We could not use footballs, touch each other, and had to stay six to eight feet apart. It was becoming extremely difficult to see any prospect of playing.

The state athletic governing body had slated the month of December as the start date for preparing for playing a season in early winter. However, we were informed that the state government of California had postponed all high school athletic contests until further notice. The winter surge and the number of COVID-19 cases spreading across the nation was increasing. We were all devastated. Uncertainty about the season was causing our players to lose hope. When Christmas break came, we stayed connected to our players, encouraging them to keep the faith and trust that a season was going to happen.

When we returned to school in January, our district said that we could not continue in-person workouts like we were doing before the break until the end of the month. It was an enormous setback for us all. We hoped that once the break was over, we could continue our workouts, with the belief we could begin practicing by the end of the month for the spring season. Our players increasingly asked why we were doing Zoom workouts with no idea when football would return. We worked extremely hard to stay positive, stay connected, and preach that we would continue until told otherwise. We resumed in-person workouts the last week of the month, but there were some dreary days in late

January and early February. Several of our senior players decided that they had had enough and quit. Feeling all hope lost, they moved on with their lives. I tried hard to keep them engaged, but I also understood where they were coming from and understood their decision. Despite the odds, some players remained hopeful.

MARCH 1, 2021

When hope of a short spring season was all but lost, the state did an about-face and created a path for us to play. If a county's positive COVID rate dropped below a certain level, they could begin preparing for an abbreviated season. This was a significant change. We progressed from a dark time to one where games were possible with optimism and hope. It didn't matter if it was one game or five; we were just elated that we were finally being given the opportunity to play games. In order to practice on Monday, March 1, every player and coach had to test negatively. We accomplished this as everyone was cleared. With this new sense of hope, we began preparing for our abbreviated spring season.

Because of the short time we had to prepare, we shortened our offensive and defensive installation plan. We perfected the fundamentals of each position. Going from pods of ten with no contact to a normal football practice was amazing. We were still doing distance learning for all academic classes, so there were no students on campus except for athletes. It was unbelievable. It elated us to resume practicing, but the logic behind everything that had happened up to this point made zero sense. We didn't argue and kept doing what we loved. They gave us two and a half weeks to prepare our team to play in our first of what would be five league games. The players, coaches, parents, and community were excited and ready to play.

Tragedy and Triumph: School Shooting, COVID-19, and League Champs

Once our first game day arrived, everyone associated with our program was beyond excited. With limited fans and all kinds of precautions in place, we began our journey of playing games. We pivoted hope into euphoria when we won the first game. However, my middle son's last season ended because of a knee injury he sustained in the game. While it was sad that he could not play, he was excited about his friend's ability to keep playing. He stayed positive, encouraging his teammates for the rest of the season. As the next few weeks progressed, we continued to win. Our team and our league rival had perfect 4-0 records going into the last game of the season. It was like a movie script. Two unbeaten teams were going to play each other for the league championship. The opposing team hadn't lost a league game since 2011 and had been the champion for 11 consecutive years. We were the last team to be outright league champs dating back to 2008. This game had huge ramifications.

As we were warming up for the game, the excitement our coaches and players felt was beyond measure. Since this was our last game, we could recognize our outgoing senior players before kickoff. As I stood there watching each player being announced, I could barely keep my emotions in check as I watched my son's name being called out. Even though he could not play, we dressed him in his uniform to feel like he was part of the team. We often encouraged injured players to dress for games so they would not feel alone and on the outside. I fought back tears, aware of his struggles for two and a half years. I had selfishly elected him to be the captain for the coin toss, which we won and, in standard fashion, deferred to the second half.

As the game began, we were not going to be denied. On our first possession, we would score and hang on to a 7-0 lead until right before halftime. It was at that point that they scored a TD, tying the game 7-7. We left the field for our halftime break. When we were leaving the field,

I asked our principal if overtime was going to be allowed. He responded with a vigorous "NO! There will be no overtime!" He said to concentrate on winning the game. Reminiscent of Cortez burning his ships upon arrival in Mexico in 1519 on their way to conquering the Aztecs, thus motivating his men, I knew what we needed to do. There simply was no turning back.

As the second half began, both teams exchanged possessions several times, with neither team scoring. Late in the 3rd quarter, we began our second offensive drive of the half, which halfway through required us to switch sides as the quarter ended. We continued to march, eventually scoring early in the 4th quarter to give us a 14-7 lead. On the next possession, our opponent drove down the field at a furious pace, getting to our own 17-yard line before fumbling the ball, which we recovered. We then marched down the field to score again, going up 21-7. The excitement on our sidelines and stands was beyond anything I had ever experienced. Victory was within reach as the game drew to a close.

On their last possession, they drove down the field to our 8-yard line. They lost yards on the first three downs and faced 4th and goal from the 13-yard line. As they dropped back to pass, we blanketed their receivers and forced their quarterback to scramble. He would ultimately reach the 5-yard line, denied entry into the end zone with less than a minute remaining in the game. As our offense took the field for the last time, we ran the clock out and secured our first outright league championship since 2008.

As our sideline exploded in celebration, I was in a state of shock, joy, and relief. The hard work and commitment of our coaches and players paid off. I found my son, hugged him tightly, and said how proud of him I was for sticking it out, even though he was injured. My eldest son, who was an assistant coach on the team, also joined in the celebration. Eventually, my wife, daughter, and mother made it to the field, where we all embraced and celebrated the monumental victory. The realization that we won and secured our first league championship in over 12 years dawned on us as we left the field. The memory is unforgettable for me and the young men who played that season.

SUMMARY OF TRAGEDY TO TRIUMPH

Several days after the game, I had time to reflect on all the challenges and adversity this group of young people had to endure. I firmly believe that the only reason our players got through everything they did was their incredible sense of resiliency. There is simply no other explanation. Their sole hope was for a better tomorrow. I like to think that we, as a coaching staff, played a minor role in preparing them for all the challenges that they faced. Tough challenges strengthened these young people for life. We expect greatness for many of the student-athletes we worked with during this period.

14

WHERE DO WE GO FROM HERE? MOVING FORWARD

"I think everybody should take the attitude that we're working to be a champion, that we want to be a champion in everything that we do. Every choice, every decision, everything that we do every day, we want to be a champion."

—Nick Saban

Following our league championship-shortened season, which ended on April 16, we took the rest of April and May off. We held our team awards ceremony in the backyard of one of our coaches' homes because of restrictions that were still in place regarding indoor gatherings. It was a glorious event as each member of the team celebrated all the accomplishments we had achieved in the past year and a half. We began working out with our returning players while also honoring the graduation of the class of 2020, which included my middle son. Following this, we began our summer practice routine to prepare for the 2021 season.

With coaching and playing sports, you can never be content with what you have accomplished in the past. The simple reason is that it's exactly that, in the past. We focused our efforts on preparing this new team for the challenges and rigors that coming fall season would bring. Only this time, we had the added target of being league champs on our back.

The school year would start in person for the first time since March 2020, which brought many fresh changes and challenges. We progressed through the pre-season with a 4-1 record before starting league play. We had a perfect 4-0 league record before playing our rival in the championship. Unfortunately, the day before the game was to be played, they had a COVID outbreak and had to cancel our game. Despite not playing, we earned our second consecutive league title and became two-time champs. We would go on to the playoffs, losing in the first round to a very talented team in a new division.

While the loss was disappointing, giving us the feeling that we had ended the season early, we were happy that we had won our league. We could celebrate our accomplishments at our team awards gathering, in which everyone shared the joys of another winning season. Following this, preparation for the 2022 season had begun.

At the time of writing this book, the Delta and Omicron variants of COVID-19 are surging in our nation. We are seeing restrictions and mandates increase despite the level of vaccinations that have taken place. We can't predict the future, but with faith and government support, we will be ready for a season.

Where Do We Go From Here? Moving forward

My goal and hope for this labor of love was to provide a blueprint for how to teach, inspire, and motivate young people to go beyond what they thought was possible. While I do not mean the ideas presented in this work to be an end-all-be-all manual on how to be a champion without winning a championship, it is what has worked for us. I hope that the content in this book will benefit you on your journey in life and that the lessons I have learned will be applicable and useful to you.

15

EPILOGUE

I began this book writing project in the spring of 2019 and ended it with the conclusion of our 2021 season. Following this, we began our preparation for the 2022 campaign. Our hopes were high, as we had several returning players from the previous season who contributed to our 2nd League Championship.

The off-season revealed multiple challenges ahead. First, our senior class of players, while extremely talented on the field, lacked leadership. I spent the bulk of my time attempting to teach leadership skills to our players but struggled to connect and get the messages I was teaching across. Second, we had some challenges on the coaching staff to fill positions and some current staff members who were not 100% on board with what we were doing. Some players weren't putting in enough effort for another championship run. Last, we had question marks at several key positions that made our job very challenging. As I worked with the players and staff from January until the start of the summer, I remained optimistic that we would be fine.

Once we entered summer, several players sustained injuries. Natural attrition caused some of these issues, while poor weight training preparation caused others. It created a situation to be creative in terms of who was playing where. While this allowed us to get several players more opportunities to participate and play, it challenged continuity.

Once we started playing games, we were struggling to accomplish our goals, but we still would win several of our games. We completed our preseason with a record of 4 wins and one loss. We entered league play and would defeat Valencia High School. It was an enormous victory for our team and program since we could not play them during the 2021 season. The next week, we lost to a very talented West Ranch team. This loss ensured it would be very difficult to win a third league championship. Things took a regrettable turn the Monday after the loss.

Our principal came to my room that morning with an email complaint about why our team was running out to take the field carrying a Blue Lives Matter flag. Traditionally, when we take the field, we have three flags that we carry out with us. One is the American flag. Another is a Saugus Strong flag. Last, we carry a pancake flag, which represents all our linemen. Unbeknownst to me, one of our players had been running out with a fourth flag, which was the Blue Lives Matter flag, for several of our earlier games. I didn't see the flag being carried out since, traditionally, I was behind our team when we took the field.

It was at this point that I began doing some research.

I wanted to know the story behind the flag and why anyone may take exception to it. The flag was simply a way to pay respect and honor to law enforcement. However, the more research I did, the more I discovered that this flag also carried some controversy with it. This includes those who believe it is the anti-Black Lives Matter flag. I also discovered that some White supremacy groups who had carried out protests across the nation had also flown this flag. I would reach out to our local law enforcement agencies to find out what their stance on the flag was. LAPD and LA County Sheriff's buildings and patrol vehicles do not allow this flag.

Next, I met with our senior football players to determine why they had elected to run out with this flag. After an hour-long meeting, I realized the only reason they elected to carry this flag out was to honor law enforcement. I hoped that the players would have said it was for honoring those brave law enforcement officers who came to help us on the day of our school shooting. But not one player could articulate this. I made the difficult decision to no longer allow players to run out with this flag. My reasons were multiple.

One extremist, had unfortunately hijacked this flag. While we support law enforcement, I could not in good conscience continue to run out with it, knowing that it offended others. Second, if we continued to run out with this flag, I would have no ground to stand on should team members want to run out with any other flags that may offend people. Third, I wanted our team to focus on playing the game as opposed to carrying out some kind of political message. Our team should accept all groups, regardless of their identity. Last, we had decided that we could recognize and honor law enforcement officers in other ways besides running out with this flag.

My decision caused a powerful response from both supporters and detractors on either side. I had not expected the backlash of law enforcement and community members that we experienced. I tried extremely hard to explain to everyone my reasons for this decision, but it didn't seem to make a difference. People felt hurt and upset because of my decision. There was a feeling that I had submitted to pressure being given by those who were against the flag. Our district would voice support by reiterating my statement. It didn't matter. Folks on both sides were extremely passionate and committed to showing their stance on the issue at our next home game. Once the game arrived, there were protestors on both sides of the issue outside our game. Both local and national news agencies were at the game. It was a circus. It was all I could do to keep our players focused on playing the game. Despite winning, the experience leading up to it strained staff and players greatly.

Following this, things seemed to die down. We could focus on playing the rest of the season with football at the front of our minds. Then, at the last league game of the season, one of our players took it upon himself to run out with the flag. He carried out the task and ran with it after the team had entered the field, despite our vigilance to prevent it. I didn't know he did this since I was preparing our kickoff team on the field. It was not until after the game they informed me of his action. I was extremely upset. Just when I thought we had moved on, the issue reared its head. The events that we experienced earlier in the season once again resumed leading up to our first-round playoff game.

The team we were playing was from a more diverse community, exacerbating the issue. They believed they were coming to a hostile environment. They were concerned about the safety of their players and parents. I called their head coach and assured him that his concerns, while maybe warranted, would be a non-issue. I explained our situation to him and made sure he understood that his players, coaches, and supporters would be safe. Everyone's focus was on playing the game.

As the week progressed, the stress of the issue took its toll on our players and coaches. No matter how hard I tried to keep everyone, including myself, focused on playing the game, we were all distracted. Before the game, I talked with their head coach on the field. I wanted to ensure everything was OK with his staff and players. He thanked me for the kindness of our support people and fans. His concerns quickly dissipated, and we played the game. Unfortunately, we lost the game. For the first time in my coaching career, I was relieved the season was over. We were all affected by this issue. I thanked our team for sticking it out and giving their best effort through this adversity.

I evaluated everything after the season ended. I took full responsibility for what happened. It was my responsibility to ensure our team didn't upset the community. I failed at this by not seeing our players running out with this flag and addressing it sooner. I will have to live with that.

As for now, we have begun preparations for the 2023 season. Our players have worked hard to move forward with the lessons learned. I am confident that we all have learned some valuable lessons that we will use for future challenges.

ACKNOWLEDGMENT

The ideas presented in this book would not have been possible without the countless individuals who provided me with a wealth of concepts, ideas, and support. Besides the people I already mentioned by name in the book, there are a few others I would like to recognize.

The most important acknowledgment must begin with my bride, Veronica. This journey to write this book started with the completion of her book, *I Found Love*. Seeing her hard work, dedication, and accomplishment inspired me to do the same. Her support and encouragement throughout this entire process enabled me to complete it. For that, I will forever be grateful.

I want to thank the following college football coaches who gave me their time throughout the years by talking to me in person, over the phone, or corresponding via email or text. Tim DeRuyter, thank you for always being a sounding board for me when it came to talking about all things related to defense. Wallie Kuchinski, thank you for sharing your brand of defense. Tim Tulloch, thank you for your insights on how to teach the game. Tyler Fenwick, thank you for helping me formulate the basis of everything related to offense. Dale Widhoff, thank you for giving me my first and only college coaching job, as well as showing me how to lead young men with integrity, grace, and class. Robert Dos Remedios, thank you for everything related to strength and conditioning. Your commitment to this aspect of building strong, explosive, and dynamic athletes has been the cornerstone of all we do with our players.

I want to thank Chris Vassuer, whose podcasts and clinics were very helpful in developing a methodology for teaching the game.

I want to thank the countless high school coaches who, over the years, have blessed me with their wealth of knowledge that has shaped many of the ideas shared in this book. While this list is by far from complete, the following have been instrumental over the years. Tony Crutchfield, Ty Gower, Adam Gaylor, Chris King, Jason Negro, Ray Gerena, Mike Leibin, Jim Benkert, Nacho Brache, Jeff Steinberg, and Matt Logan, thank you for all your help and support over the years.

To my Saugus family, I would like to thank Jim Klipfel, who, as my social science department chair, has inspired me to be not only a better teacher, but a better man.

Thank you to Bill Bolde and Kevin Miner, who hired me as a young head coach in 2003. Marcus Garrett and Rich Bahr, both former coaches on my staff and, later, school administrators, thank you for your never-ending support and help, especially when I got myself into trouble.

To Vince Ferry, thank you for your support and leadership, especially during our darkest days at Saugus.

To the many coaches who worked with me on our staff here at Saugus, both past and present, thank you. John Lutz, Tom Lovell, Jeff Watkins, Scott Monson, and Marc Zimmerman, thank you all for influencing me and sharing our successes and challenges over the years.

Finally, to Dave Russell, who has been with me since being hired at Saugus, thank you for your dedication, commitment, and friendship.

Acknowledgment

I want to thank my high school teammates, Jeff Cortez and Andy Kaminski, who joined me in the ranks of coaching high school football. Their love and support over the years have been a continuous source of help, inspiration, and a sounding board as it pertains to coaching and balance in life.

Part of this job involves media coverage, most of which has been through newspaper articles. I want to thank Gerry Gittleson, Cary Osborne, Eric Sodheimer, and Tarrak Fattal, whose writing and reporting on our program over the years has been excellent.

Coaching a high school football team requires tremendous support from our parents. Thank you to everyone who participated in our booster club, the Saugus Gridiron Club.

I want to thank my family members whose love and support throughout my career have allowed me to do what I love to do. To my children, thank you for being my foundation.

Thank you to my mom, Susan, my Aunt Nancy, my sisters Tiffany and Kim, and their husbands and children.

Thank you to my wife's large family, brothers, and sister-in-law.

Finally, I would like to thank all the past and present players I have been blessed to serve. From my first year starting at Village Christian High School to my time at John Muir High School and Canyon High School to my college position at Occidental College, this job would not have been possible or rewarding with the players that I was able to coach. Thank you all for trusting me to be your coach. I will forever be in debt to you and will always be your coach.

ABOUT THE AUTHOR

Jason Bornn is not just a football coach; he is a mentor, a leader, and a firm believer in the transformative power of sports. With an impressive 35-year coaching career under his belt, including 22 years as the Head Coach of Saugus High School in Santa Clarita, California, Coach Bornn has left an indelible mark on the lives of countless young athletes. His journey in the world of football is nothing short of remarkable, characterized by dedication, perseverance, and an unwavering commitment to shaping the character of his players.

In his two-decade tenure at Saugus High School, Coach Bornn has achieved a record of 121 wins and 109 losses, a testament to his ability to lead his team to success consistently. His accomplishments include four Foothill League titles in 2008, 2011, 2020, and 2021 and an impressive 13 playoff appearances in the past 22 seasons. Coach Bornn guided his team to four CIF-Semi Final appearances in 2016, 2013, 2008, and 2007.

However, Coach Bornn's impact extends far beyond the scoreboard. He firmly believes that the football field is a classroom for life lessons. Through coaching, he instills in his players essential skills such as commitment, discipline, perseverance, integrity, and self-belief. He understands that these attributes are not just valuable in the context of a game but are fundamental to success in all aspects of life.

Coach Bornn strongly emphasizes team building and leadership training, recognizing that these skills are essential for the gridiron and personal and professional growth. He encourages players to strive for excellence and give their best in every endeavor. His philosophy is simple yet profound: success is achieved when a player can look in the mirror at the end of the day, knowing they have given their all and have nothing to be ashamed of. Before his tenure at Saugus High School, Coach Bornn honed his coaching expertise at various institutions in California, including Occidental College in Eagle Rock, Canyon High School in Santa Clarita, John Muir High School in Pasadena, and Village Christian High School in Sun Valley. These experiences enriched his coaching style and helped him develop a holistic approach to mentoring young athletes.

Coach Bornn's educational background further underscores his commitment to excellence. He earned a Bachelor of Science in History from California State University Northridge while serving as a reservist in the United States Marine Corps stationed in Long Beach. His pursuit of knowledge didn't stop there; he later earned a Master's Degree in Educational Administration from Point Loma University.

Beyond the football field and his coaching career, Coach Bornn enjoys a fulfilling personal life. He and his lovely wife, Veronica, reside in Santa Clarita, where they share their lives with their three adult children, Angelo, Julian, and Paloma. Away from the gridiron, Coach Bornn cherishes quality time with his family, indulges in vacation adventures, explores the world through reading, and savors the pleasures of dining out.

In summary, Jason Bornn is not just a Head Coach; he is a man who embodies the principles of commitment, discipline, perseverance,

About the Author

integrity, and belief in one's potential. His journey through the world of football has been marked by success on the field and a profound impact on it. His story serves as a testament to the enduring power of sports in shaping character and teaching life's most valuable lessons. Coach Bornn's legacy will continue to inspire and empower generations of young athletes for years to come.

APPENDIX

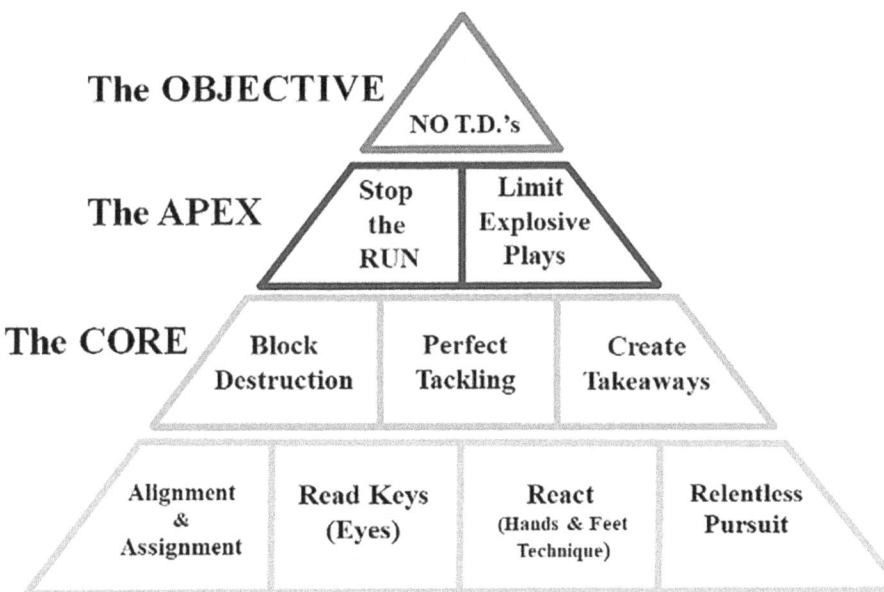

OFFENSIVE PYRAMID OF SUCCESS

The OBJECTIVE: SCORE

The APEX: 4 yards on Run Plays | Catch Every Ball on Pass Plays

The CORE: Finish Blocks | Execute Explosive Plays | Protect The Ball

The FOUNDATION: Knowledge (Alignment, Assignment, and Plays) | Aggression | Fundamentals By Position | Relentless Effort

www.ingramcontent.com/pod-product-compliance
Lightning Source LLC
Chambersburg PA
CBHW051614010526
44107CB00036B/1420/J